# Shiftability

# Shiftability

Creating a Sustainable Competitive Advantage in Selling

Mitch Little & Hendre Coetzee

ISBN: 1541001648
ISBN 13: 9781541001640
Library of Congress Control Number: 2016920563
CreateSpace Independent Publishing Platform
North Charleston, South Carolina

"Do you agree that sales is undergoing a crisis of confidence in these rapidly changing times? Then *Shiftability* is the book you need now. It will show you how to transform your thinking, sharpen your skills, and master the changing environment of sales."
— Daniel H. Pink, Author of *To Sell Is Human*

"A brilliant treatise combining a shift -- perhaps even a transformation -- of both mindset and skillset that is absolutely imperative for a sales professional to acquire in our ever-changing world of sales. Really, this book is a masterpiece!"
— Bob Burg, Co-author of *The Go-Giver*

"*Shiftability* dives deep into the heart of intelligent, collaborative selling. The powerful, inspired takeaways herein can lift any salesperson's performance to surprising new levels...this book is paradoxically ahead of its time and immediately useful."
— Steve Chandler, Author of *Time Warrior*

"From mindset to skillset *Shiftability* gives you actionable, practical, doable steps that give the ultimate competitive advantage in sales and in life. Don't just read this book – use this book!"
— Anthony Parinello, Author of *Selling to VITO: The Very Important Top Officer*

"Everything about buying and selling has changed---except the sales person. Mitch and Hendre focus on the mindset shifts that are critical to success in today's new world of sales."
— David A. Brock, Author of *Sales Manager Survival Guide*

"With Mitch and Hendre at your side—given their incredible experience and expertise in both selling solutions and coaching behavior change—you have in *Shiftability* the personal guide necessary to make truly transformational change in both mindset and skillset."
— Brent Adamson, Author of *The Challenger Sale* and *The Challenger Customer*

*To my Anneke and Nikka –*
*You are my rhythm and anchors. I cannot thank you both enough for the sacri-*
*fices that you have made and faith that you have in me. Better together - Ons*
*saam.*
*Hendre*


*To my wife Jeanie –*
*Thank you is not enough and yet I will say it. It is our togetherness and your love*
*that has always made a difference for me. Our journey together has proven time*
*and time again that soul mates do exist. Thank you for being mine!*
*Mitch*

# Table of Contents

# Foreword

As I travel around the world supporting companies' efforts to adopt the principles laid out in *The Challenger Sale*, I'm often struck by the importance not just of what our research at CEB says, but how that story is told. Tell the story right, and you see excitement, curiosity, open-mindedness, and a willingness to give it a try. Tell it wrong, and you're just as likely to meet resistance, fear, suspicion, and even anger.

Yet, in either case, the underlying data never changes. Sales professionals most aligned with "Challenger" behaviors are far more likely to be star performers, while those hewing more closely to "Relationship Builder" behaviors are much more likely struggle.

Why would the exact same data provoke such radically different reactions among arguably very similar populations? It turns out, positioning is everything. If, for example, sales reps perceive Challenger largely as a story of "You're doing it wrong, and I'm here to 'fix' you," you're almost certainly doomed to struggle. Effectively, that is a story of accusation, more than empowerment: "This is *your* fault, and *I'm* here to make *you* better." Understandably, a message like that is going to meet resistance, if not outright rejection. It's demoralizing, even threatening. And in many cases, it's also actually wrong.

If, however, one positions the story differently—removing the "blame" from reps themselves and placing the need for change instead at the feet of a changing world, the message resonates far more strongly. In this case, a sales rep's past success is acknowledged, even honored, but then placed in the context of a rapidly changing world of customer buying behavior that will likely threaten that success heading into the future. As I like to put it, "Let me show you what happens when we take the old world of selling and run it right into the teeth of the new world of buying. Things fall apart. Not because we're selling poorly, but because customers are buying differently."

Notice, the punch line here isn't "You're doing it wrong, and I'm here to fix you," but rather, "You're doing it right, but we need to evolve." In the first version, the rep is "wrong," and in the second, they're "right." But the fundamental story is the exact same either way, Challengers still win.

Why does this matter? Well, it turns out, it matters a lot. After all, we're ultimately talking about shifting human behavior—sometimes dramatically. And as the authors of *Shiftability* tell us, it's extremely difficult for us to change what we *do*, if we don't first change what we *believe*. Any effective and lasting change in skillset must first begin with an equally fundamental shift in *mindset*. And in *Shiftability*, Mitch Little and Hendre Coetzee offer sales professionals a practical, step-by-step guide for first acknowledging and then achieving that shift.

So while we spend much of our time at CEB speaking of the "changing commercial landscape," Mitch and Hendre dive deep in the opposite direction, turning instead inward to ask, "What have you done to adapt? Not just what you do, but how you think and what you believe." In many ways it's the pre-work for truly transformational change. And with Mitch and Hendre at your side—given their incredible experience and expertise in both selling solutions and coaching behavior change—you have in *Shiftability* the personal guide necessary to make that change.

Crucially, however, that guidance isn't simply a familiar appeal for "openness to change," but a nuanced and powerful set of tools to help sales professionals think both critically and systematically about what to *change* and what to *keep*. As Mitch and Hendre put it, the mindset of shiftability "is about awareness and action, giving and taking, while staying true to who you are, rooted in principles of integrity and purpose. Shiftability responds to outward demands from inward strength, purpose and skill."

And it is that "inward strength" that they're seeking to build here, not just practically, but inspirationally as well.

Along the way they're careful to lay out and explain a number of lessons crucial to applying a shiftability mindset to complex sales:

1. **Your biggest limitation is mindset, not skillset:** Without careful, frank exploration of one's "limiting beliefs" sales professionals are likely to struggle to effectively appreciate or adopt important, new sales behaviors.

2. **Selling is fundamentally a human interaction:** While new skills matter—and matter a lot—they're only effective when applied through the oldest and most important attributes of effective human interaction: empathy, connection, and listening.

3. **Effective customer insight isn't "presented," it's co-created:** While providing customers with insight about their business is the heart and soul of effective selling in the new world, that insight is far more powerful when created collaboratively *with* customers rather than simply delivered *to* them.

4. **Complexity is an opportunity:** Far from something to be avoided or mitigated, complexity proves to be a powerful tool, wielded skillfully by the best sales reps, to position both themselves and their customers for far greater success than otherwise possible by avoiding it altogether.

5. **Tension is a tool:** An important tool in fact. Like complexity, creating a certain amount of "constructive tension" as part of a complex sale is crucial for driving the kind of change necessary to overcome the inertia of customers' current status quo.

These are just some of the critical lessons at the heart of a shiftability mindset. Of course, there are many other, equally important concepts, ideas, and ah-ha moments along the way, accompanied by practical exercises and powerful tools for reflection. But I'll leave you to discover those on your own. When you put it all together, I think you'll find *Shiftability* to be a quick read with a lasting impact. I very much enjoyed it, and I hope that you do to.

Brent Adamson
Author of *The Challenger Sale* and *The Challenger Customer*

Introduction

# As We Begin ...

**A**nyone in sales today faces an uncertain future. We could almost say anyone in any business role today faces an uncertain future. We live in an age of disruption and disintermediation. The business landscape is rapidly and radically changing and it keeps getting harder to predict what lies ahead.

Sales methodologies are changing as well, partly in response to the flux in the business environment. Through the valuable work and research of many in the field we understand the nature of the buying and selling relationship differently.

All of this uncertainty around us raises an important question:

The sales context has changed.

Selling methodologies are changing.

*Have you changed?*

What we see today is sales professionals responding to all of the movement around them by switching companies, or changing roles, and of course attempting to change the way they do things. Because this is how human beings respond when faced with a problem: *Okay, what do I have to do to fix this?* We get asked this all the time in our coaching and managing of sales teams: **Yes, everything is changing. What should we do?**

The assumption is if we just do the right things, we will have the right results and then we will be successful. Perhaps you have thought this way too and tried to change things around you and the way you do things. Likely you have found yourself in the same place, getting the same results, running up against the same frustrations. And we have to ask—what is the common denominator? The answer is you.

You can change your job, change your boss, change your city, and try a new method, but unless you undergo a personal transformation yourself, all of these external changes in context and methodology are not going to get you where you need to go or help you become who you need to be in order to have success in a complex new world

Deepak Chopra said, "I am not a human thinking, I am not a human doing, I'm a human *being*." When we try to do the right things in order to get the right results, expecting to then be successful, we are saying that we are "human doings."

Instead, we need to start with who we are and what we believe. Human beings act out of their beliefs and sense of purpose; what we do is a result of what we believe. If I believe that I can make a sale, I will do all the work that is necessary to make that sale. If I believe that things are going to get difficult, then things are most likely going to get difficult. We become our own self-fulfilling prophecy.

So one of the invitations we'd like to make in this book is for you to recognize that what you believe - about your context, about the future, about selling - determines how you engage. If you are afraid, then you are going to act and do things a fearful person does.

So before you change what you do, first we need to explore what you believe and how much of what you are doing is determined by fear, concern or limited ways of thinking. This is where personal transformation starts.

This personal transformation is necessary to solve the challenge facing every sales professional today: how do I stay relevant in this new world, navigate the shifting environment around me, and deliver value to both my client and my company?

Through our work guiding and coaching sales organizations we have been applying the leading research in selling and teaching some important new methods. In particular, we acknowledge the groundbreaking work of *The Challenger Sale* and the imperative to Teach, Tailor and Take Control. *Challenger* has provoked an important debate about the real value a salesperson delivers to the customer today, and the principles of *Challenger* are at the core of what we teach. Daniel Pink's book *Drive* and the premise that autonomy, mastery and purpose are central to success today has also been highly influential, along with several other works.

But we have learned that before we can equip sales teams with new methods and train them to do things like Teach, Tailor and Take Control, we first need to help them develop a different mindset and address this question of personal transformation. To maximize sales effectiveness today and truly impact your client you must have a difference-making methodology **and** a transformation in mindset and beliefs. It is the aggregate combination of both that will supercharge your outcomes. The right shift in mindset makes it possible to truly understand, internalize and act upon groundbreaking methodologies.

Through this book, we invite you to start a journey of personal transformation that will equip you with this mindset that you need to thrive in the current shifting context and survive whatever future changes lie ahead.

First, we will explore what you believe. We will help you identify and overcome the limiting beliefs that are keeping you back. We will take a look at your purpose and motivation and show you how staying focused on your true north produces better results than focusing simply on results. When you shift your beliefs and get excited and are willing to engage, then you will be ready to **do** new things and achieve new and improved better results!

In the second part of the book, we will discuss the core skillset sales professionals need to excel in selling today. These six core skills are anchored in the mindset shift of part one. Some of these skillset shifts may seem a bit counterintuitive. For example, we believe it is vital to welcome and embrace complexity rather than constantly drive to simplification. Similarly, we don't want you to remove tension, but learn to manage it and leverage it toward action.

Making shifts like these will only be possible because first you will have understood the beliefs that hold you back from making them and adopted a mindset that will help you be nimble with new methods.

We believe all of this is wrapped up in a quality we have termed **shiftability**. Shiftability encompasses both awareness and action. It is having the combined mindset and skillset to understand the circumstances around you and then to act appropriately in pursuit of your desired results. Shiftability is about adapting and changing in response to circumstances around you – but it's not about compromise.

Bruce Lee said, "Notice that the stiffest tree is most easily cracked, while the bamboo or the willow survives by bending with the wind." The tree that bends with the wind is rooted in the ground. It bends but it does not blow away.

Compromise, or merely being shifty, means that you simply succumb to pressures around you. Rather, shiftability is about awareness and action, giving and taking, while staying true to who you are, rooted in principles of integrity and purpose. Shiftability responds to outward demands from inward strength, purpose and skill.

The mindset of shiftability acknowledges the need for change and transformation and embraces it, keeping an open mind about new ideas while wisely retaining things that still apply, always learning, always building, always growing.

The skillset of shiftability will vary depending on your context. The shiftability skillset for sales professionals includes:

- mastering situational client engagement,
- embracing conflict,
- creating and delivering personalized insight,
- managing and leveraging tension,
- asking for the business and sustaining client engagement,
- and not being afraid of NO.

We believe shiftability is a quality that you can cultivate and develop. In fact, we will be so bold as to say that it is a quality that you must cultivate and develop to stay relevant and succeed in selling today. That's why we wrote this book.

By the end of this book, you will not just have another sales process or methodology. Instead you will be equipped to set out on the road to relevance along with your entire client engagement team—inside sales, outside sales, technical support, management, marketing, product development, and customer service.

Today's sales leaders must make a major transformation. Sales leaders must transform from being product and solution experts with technical skills to being client engagement project managers with strong interpersonal skills who can deliver the appropriate resources at the right time to help the client in the best way.

Are you ready? Let's begin with how we got here in the first place ...

One

# The Elephants Aren't Just In The Room – They Are Everywhere

## HOW DID WE GET HERE? WHERE ARE WE HEADED?

If you do not change direction,
you may end up where you are heading.

*Lao Tzu*

To improve is to change; to be perfect is to change
often.

*Winston Churchill*

I t seems impossible that three tons of mammoth power can creep up on you without a sound. But any who have encountered elephants in the wild will know this to be true. Elephants can be incongruously stealthy, scary quiet, and seemingly appear from nowhere, suddenly emerging in full view with intimidating presence and power.

In 1993 Hendre was with a group of students on a road trip up through Africa. The group had traveled through Lusaka in Zambia and stopped along the Zambezi River to visit the Victoria Falls. That afternoon they took a sunset cruise on the Zambezi River about a mile upstream from the Falls. There are very few things as amazing as an African sunset and seeing huge crocodiles just a few feet from the boat. The river at this point is about a half-mile wide and has a number of tiny islands where lazy crocodiles soak up the afternoon sun with their jaws wide open. The boat captain would get precariously close for a better view of the crocodiles – so close in fact that the boat would enter a number of areas that were overgrown with bamboo reeds and leaves.

As Hendre leaned over to get a better look at a sunbathing crocodile, suddenly an elephant trunk raised up inches in front of him. An elephant was the last thing he expected to see in the middle of the Zambezi River just above Victoria Falls. How did it get there?

When we refer to "the elephant in the room" we are usually talking about the fact that we are avoiding the obvious because we are too afraid of addressing the issue. The funny thing is that we never notice how the elephant enters the room. In selling, several elephants have crept up on us in recent times. Suddenly we find ourselves confronted with challenges and changes that can make us question the very role we are in. Is there still a place for the sales professional in business?

In business, as on a safari, we miss seeing the elephant most often because we are looking elsewhere. Sales people are busy doing what we have always done and what worked the last time that we simply haven't noticed the shifting environment and the elephants around us until they are right in front of us. The current reality of our world is that there are so many changes happening all at once that people often have change fatigue and choose to only focus on what they already know and ignore the elephants in the room. It requires a huge commitment to embrace the ambiguity and engage in this context of uncertainty. There are elephants everywhere. How did they get here?

\*\*\*

**In the beginning there were people who** made stuff and people who needed stuff. Then there were the peddlers of stuff who helped the makers and the buyers find each other.

The peddlers of stuff were very successful for hundreds of years, because the makers and buyers needed them. Stuff was bought and sold and everyone was okay.

Then things changed.

## THAT WAS THEN ...

It was a typically warm and sunny Arizona day. The cloudless blue skies seemed to go on forever as Mitch drove across the desert out of Phoenix on one of his monthly sales trips to Las Vegas. This time was a bit different. Mitch's usual mode of transportation was his bright silver Audi 5000T. This day he was behind the wheel of a bright orange and white rental truck from U-Haul.

The two-ton box on wheels was loaded front to back and fully to the ceiling with high tech data. But this was not data as we think of it today. This was technical product information contained in hundreds of copies of technical documents, printed and bound in books from various manufacturers. These were called data books. In the technical sales trade they were almost as good as gold. Electrical engineers would go to almost any means needed to get their hands on their favorite manufacturers' data books.

And Mitch had an entire truckload of them.

He was on his way to a government contractor in Nevada. This was a tough account to get into to talk with even just a few of their thousands of engineers. But Mitch had found that if he set up shop in the parking lot with a truckload of data books, over a couple of days nearly every engineer in the company would come out to visit him. They could pick and choose from any of the dozens of manufacturers that he represented and take any data books they needed. All he asked was that they grant him access at a later date. Through Mitch's semi-annual book drive he built one heck of a contact Rolodex.

This was 1977 and the electronics industry was in its infancy. Apple Computer had just incorporated, Star Wars had just opened and set new records, and Elvis had just left the building. At the time Mitch was a Field Sales Engineer working for Wyle Electronics, one of the largest distributors of electronic components in the industry. They represented and sold semiconductors for Motorola, Intel, Fairchild and many others. They also sold a variety of electromechanical products like connectors and switches and passive products such as capacitors. Wyle represented the best of the best.

In these early days of the electronics industry a sales person working in the distribution world was viewed as a great source of information. Customers eagerly welcomed sales reps whether they were bringing in data books or doughnuts. At that time the only real source of technical product information was the printed material that the various manufacturers created. There was no Internet. This was a time known as BCP (Before Cell Phones). Electronic messages between companies were sent through a system called a TWX or a Telex. Fax machines were just becoming real. The human was the primary means of conveying the realities of the fast moving electronics industry.

Every Monday night after work Mitch's sales team would meet with various manufacturers over pizza and beer and hear all about what wonderful new technologies and products they were about to bring to market. They would check out the new technical literature and sometimes they would even score the ever-elusive "sample" that they could deliver to a really important client.

Life was grand and the role of sales professionals had maximum meaning and purpose. They were the kings and queens of data. Not just data, but data everything. They had data sheets, data books, data libraries, and data brochures. They had copies of advertising, which was just more data. They had product data, solution data, reliability data, and eventually, data CDs.

Not only did sales reps have all of the data known to the technical world, but they also had free products they called samples. They had samples to hand out for specific client projects, they had sample kits, they had product sample packs and solution sample packs. They even had product demo boards, product evaluation kits, and full demo system solutions. They had development systems and emulation tools. And even more importantly the sales rep had CONTROL of it. It was theirs to gift to their favorite clients, theirs to spread out, move around and use to build relationships.

Sales reps also had control of the feedback on the use of the products and samples. They controlled the communication to the client and the communication back to the manufacturer of the products. The sales rep had it all – all the data, all the products, and all of the control.

That was then …

## THIS IS NOW …

Flash forward to today.

The electronics industry is thriving, the Star Wars franchise is still going strong, Apple is one of the premier companies in the world, and today the sales professional is on the verge of leaving the building.

We are no longer the kings and queens of data. Our customers do not need us to bring them information. They have the Internet for that. A revolution of massive disruption and disintermediation is underway.

And this changes everything.

A CEB study of more than 1,400 B2B customers across different industries revealed that 57% of a typical purchase decision today is made before a customer even talks to a supplier.

This means that in a decision-making process that starts with an idea and ends with the purchasing of product, today's buyer typically does not engage with a sales person until they are 57% of the way through the entire cycle. They have independently researched and gathered their own information. Buyers have already assessed nearly all of the needs, prioritized the capabilities, compared and benchmarked the suppliers, and have researched pricing.

This is a really ugly spot for a salesperson to come into the picture for the first time. About the only things left to discuss are price and delivery—not an easy place to differentiate or add value!

More recent surveys of the same subject suggest that 57% is actually an optimistic number. It is more likely that your customers are only reaching out to their suppliers when they are about 75% of the way through the entire process. Now we are talking about coming in even later in the process with even less opportunity to differentiate.

The modern sales professional is fighting to stay relevant to both their customers and to their organizations. Nobody is running to greet us in the lobby, hoping to get one of our precious databooks. We are no longer the gatekeepers of information.

Obsolescence and irrelevance are looming on the horizon. In fact, some are already proclaiming the death of the salesman. And there's more bad news.

Along with the paradigm shifts in the control and flow of information there has been a seismic shift in the nature of the procurement process itself. The commoditization of information through the Internet has contributed to the recent resurgence of a particular style of aggressive supply chain management, popular in the eighties under the benign-sounding moniker, PICOS.

## A MAN NAMED JOSÉ

In March 1989 Tim Berners-Lee wrote a proposal for what would become the Worldwide Web. Nine months later the first commercial Internet service provider in the United States served its first customer. At the same time as the modern Internet was emerging, a man named José Ignacio López de Arriortúa was revolutionizing procurement at General Motors.

During his tenure, Lopez was nicknamed "Super Lopez" for his wizardry in cost reduction and streamlining production. His system was called PICOS (Program for the Implementation and Cost Optimization of Suppliers, sometimes noted as Purchased Input Cost Optimization). In theory, the PICOS system was designed to "help" a supplier reduce its costs so it could "share" those cost reductions with GM. In reality, it was a system designed to defeat weak supplier negotiation and their entire management team.

PICOS is a process by which the buyer personally and emotionally bludgeons the seller into a corner whereby all of the seller's products and services are devalued and dedifferentiated to a point where they are nothing more than simple commodities, and the only thing that will make them stand out from all of the competition is their lower price.

While the PICOS history is colored by Lopez's defection from GM to Volkswagen in 1992 amidst charges that he stole GM secrets, and his subsequent indictment for industrial espionage, the practice remains alive and well today across most industries. Over the past three years we have seen an epidemic spread of the practice, sometimes under names like "cost optimization" or "supply systems management."

The win-win collaborative rhetoric of PICOS sounds good in theory, but in reality it is a devastating business practice. The objective is to beat the supplier into submission and to secure long-term major price reductions, and to get those commitments made for several years at a continually decreasing price. Today's PICOS teams are averaging a 10% annual price reduction target, with the aggressive teams pushing for 25% reduction.

The supply chain professionals who deploy PICOS understand how to play the "win-win relationship" card and back the supplier into a seemingly uncaring corner. They keep the individual pressure up, implying a lack of commitment to partnership for those suppliers who will not cooperate and agree to their targets. They use heavy-handed threats of escalation and manipulate the supply side of the table with every known trick in the book. It is a game with old, well-documented rules. Here is a direct excerpt from Lopez:

Section 6...
- f) Be prepared indirectly and under pressure to *bluff and lie.*
- g) *Destabilize* each supplier's people with many urgent meetings and many demands for information.
- h) Set new deadlines for suppliers to meet but defer decisions to *increase their anxiety.* [1]

In a PICOS negotiation, the sales professional is personally, professionally, and emotionally challenged at every turn.

---

1  Mack Hanan, *Sales Shock! The End of Selling Products - The Rise of CoManaging Customers,* American Management Association, 1998, pp. 24-26. Emphasis added

So, not only is today's sales professional struggling to stay relevant in the age of commoditized information, they are often being bloodied and beaten at the table by aggressive tactics of manipulation and intimidation masquerading as collaboration for the win-win deal.

## IT SEEMS A LITTLE FLAT

In many respects the rise of aggressive supply management is also due to the fact that many of today's sales and purchasing practices are rooted in business economics of the past. Forty years ago 10% to 20% growth per year in revenue was pretty much the norm for most industries. And this growth was sustained for a long time. Year after year, revenue and profits continued to rise and most of us assumed this would be the norm forever. We created compensation plans, sales practices, purchasing styles, and operational standards in almost every category based on endless growth. This became the baseline for all things.

Well, those times have come and gone, and today the world is flat in terms of growth globally. It may shift and ebb regionally, but the fundamental growth of the world's economy is simply not what it was when the rules that most of us follow today for selling in the B2B environment were set in place.

This lack of growth has many implications. The environment of the public company is driven by growth, and mostly by growth in terms of profitability. Companies, public or private, only have two knobs to control for generating profits: revenue and cost. Not too complex.

However, the notion of control is perhaps questionable. In reality, the fundamental of revenue growth is not totally in a company's control, since their customer base has a strong influence over revenue, which is a huge uncontrolled variable. So, the hard truth is that the only knob that a company can actually control is cost. This cost control element has landed primarily right in the lap of the procurement organizations in every company. Procurement, purchasing, supply chain management, buyers, sourcing, vendor management—teams by many names are all focused on reducing product costs.

Cost reduction has just as many names: piece price variance or PPV, annual cost downs, enhanced supplier relationships, preferred supplier programs, supplier score carding, vendor ratings, gold/silver/bronze partnership programs, win-win negotiations, and a host of others. All of these teams, programs and practices are aimed at one thing—lower prices.

This trifecta of commoditized information and disintermediation, widespread aggressive cost-reduction and use of PICOS-style negotiation, and a flat-growth economic environment, makes things difficult for sales professionals today. There is a new urgency to figuring out how to stay relevant, how to stand up and push back to return the sales conversation to value with the right people, and to discovering how to operate in today's economy.

The landscape of selling has changed dramatically and it continues to change rapidly. How do you navigate this uncharted territory? How do you chart a course through this changing landscape? You have to learn how to shift ...

Shift into different abilities.

Shift onto a new plane of performance.

Shift into a deeper understanding of value and your role in creating it.

Shift into a new mindset.

Shift into a new skillset.

Most of all, you have to be willing to shift and choose to move forward, even though the way is not clear. You have to cultivate shiftability.

## SO I HAVE TO CHANGE—AGAIN?

Juggling her coffee and her laptop, Kristine pushed open the door to the conference room with her elbow, a few minutes late for the weekly division sales meeting. As she made her way to her seat she caught Dave's eye. He made a small nod to the right. She followed his gaze. Three stacks of bright colored hardcover books occupied center stage. Kristine's stomach knotted and she looked back to Dave. He smirked and rolled his eyes.

Whatever it was, Kristine knew a couple of things for sure. There would be a few good ideas to get excited about but she would probably be told to abandon a few old ideas that had worked for her in order to get with the new program. And Dave would make some good beer money again, selling everyone's new books on eBay.

Sound familiar? Perhaps your sales manager handed you this book to read over the weekend and told you to come back Monday ready to discuss it in your sales meeting. Please don't sell it on eBay just yet.

Kristine's sales manager, like so many others, is frantically trying to solve this problem: **How does a sale professional stay relevant today?** How do we equip ourselves to be successful in aggressive PICOS-style negotiations? How do we make sure we deliver value to our organization? To our clients? And ultimately, to ourselves?

So we are eagerly searching for the next best technique in selling, adopting and mandating new methods, changing focus, trying different incentives, and designing new programs. We get very busy doing new things, something, anything. But too often, even though we have changed everything, we get the same old results. We knock our heads up against the same problems and find ourselves right back where we started, still on the edge of irrelevance.

The whole effort becomes change for change's sake, without any real progress or improvement made. Several key misconceptions underpin this cycle of change that doesn't change anything.

## OUT WITH THE OLD, IN WITH THE NEW

The first misconception is that a shift or change is always an either/or proposition. We will either adopt this new program wholeheartedly and abandon our previous methods OR we will reject this new idea and stubbornly stick to the old plan.

Neil Rackham, author of *SPIN Selling*, calls this the "Armageddon selling formula" and describes it like this.

"Everything you've ever learned about sales is wrong and, unless you stop doing it instantly, your sales efforts will shortly die in agony. There is, however, one simple cure that I have discovered. It is..." and here the author puts in a pitch for the appropriate magic bullet, such as "my prospecting method," "my selection system," "our funnel management process," or "our trademarked social media analytics"—take your pick ...[2]

This is probably the biggest failing of many sales formulas and usually what inspires controversy. The champions enthusiastically adopt the new program and throw out everything they have been doing up to this point. The detractors disdainfully reject the new ideas completely because they are unwilling to part with their old ways. In both cases change is understood to be a net-zero exchange, instead of a process of building, growth and evolution.

In this book we would like to suggest that shifting is not binary, but instead mostly a both/and proposition. You will need to learn new skills, apply new ideas in selling, AND still maintain the old ideas that work well but perhaps understand and apply them in new ways. We don't want you to abandon methods and skills that are successful for you. We also don't want you reject new ideas just because they are new and perhaps not yet proven in your own experience.

The challenge becomes choosing which changes to adopt, and which shifts to make.

We aim to show you a framework for putting the best of today's thinking in selling into practice. We are going to help you navigate your way through the noise to six essentials shifts we believe you need to make to stay relevant and be effective. But first we need to help you answer this pressing question: *How do I make changes that stick?*

## TO DO, OR NOT TO DO?

The second misconception about change is that it is all about doing. When we are faced with a problem, usually our first thought is, what should I do to solve this problem? Then we get very busy doing things to solve our problem. We think that if we could just change our behavior, develop a new skill, apply a new technique, or start a new program, then surely we will be more successful. Hence the flood of books on selling that promise new ways to **do** sales.

---

2  From the Foreword to *Insight Selling* by Mike Schultz and John Doerr.

We are going to show you why doing isn't the right place to start for sustainable change. Rather, we need to start with changing who we are at the core in our beliefs, not just changing our techniques.

Before we get to showing you the things you can do that will help put you on the road to success as a sales professional today, we need to talk to you about your being. In order to **do** something different, you have to **believe** something different.

This is the heart of transformation. And, transformation is exactly what is required.

Part 1

# Shifting Our Mindset

Our mindset is how our beliefs translate into our thinking and ultimately into our actions. Carol Dweck, in her book *Mindset – The New Psychology of Success*, describes powerful framework for us to consider how we relate to our context, our opportunities and ourselves. Dweck makes a distinction between a **fixed mindset** versus a **growth mindset**. If we hold limiting beliefs about ourselves and our business we inevitably will engage in activities that are congruent with these very beliefs – a fixed mindset. You can learn all kinds of new skills and start using new technology but if your mindset is set in an old way of thinking, the new skills and new technology will be abandoned in a short amount of time. The way you believe determines how you think and how you think determines how you act. In contrast, a growth mindset looks at the world from a learner's perspective. From this vantage point you can explore and engage new contexts and shifting environments with less resistance and more curiosity.

Developing shiftability starts with our mindset.

# Two

# Change and Transformation

## OVERCOMING LIMITING BELIEFS

The secret of change is to focus all your energy,
not on fighting the old,
but on building the new.

SOCRATES

What got you here, won't get you there.

MARSHALL GOLDSMITH

**P**hoenix artist **Ted Love takes old cigar boxes and** clothing and creates unique pieces. He started with making jewelry boxes and then expanded to making charging stations, lamps and other one-of-a-kind home goods. He especially enjoys creating very personal memorial boxes for clients, perhaps using a shirt from a loved one, or a favorite concert t-shirt.

Ted is an upcycler, committed to using recycled, salvaged and found materials in his jewelry and art pieces. "I've always found new uses for old items and looked at things in a different way," he says. "I've always been able to give new value to things others have discarded."

Upcycling is a type of recycling but with a different focus. Recycling takes consumer products and breaks them down to recover value from the materials like plastic, glass and paper. Upcycling seeks to create new value by taking old or discarded things and turning them into something better, usually more useful or more beautiful.

Often, the changes are truly remarkable. And sometimes the original item is transformed completely.

Some things are *changed*, while others are truly *transformed*. What is the difference?

## THE NATURE OF A THING

Let's imagine we picked up a chair from the thrift store and we are going to change it - we are going to become upcyclers. What might we do?

We could sand it down and give it a fresh coat of paint. Then we could change the upholstery and recover the seat in leather. If we were feeling ambitious we might put taller legs on it to use it as a barstool. Or we could add casters to make it a rolling desk chair.

At the end of our efforts we would have a changed chair. It would probably be more useful and perhaps a little bit more beautiful. However, with all these changes it is still basically the same thing. The fundamental purpose of the thing has been preserved: it is still a chair intended for sitting.

Now, what if we set out to transform the chair, instead of just change it? We would take all the parts that collectively made the chair and imagine another use or purpose for it. We could take the legs off the chair, build a frame, add some wheels and an engine and we will have a created a go-kart. We will have transformed the chair from a piece of furniture into a vehicle. We have shifted the purpose of the thing we started with.

Change gives you more or perhaps a better version of the same thing. Transformation, however, is a shift in purpose.

If we are to adapt to the rapidly changing world we are working in, we need to be transformed, not just changed.

## TRANSFORMATION AND SELLING

The world of the sales person is transforming and transforming rapidly. We know it and feel it all around us. In an environment where there is significant upheaval we don't want to get left behind. We want to keep pace with the twists and turns and we can end up making hasty decisions just to meet the perceived demand of the day. Unfortunately, we don't always take the time to look at the fundamentals that have led to the shift in the first place.

The trends in sales that we have observed and described are the surface level effects of the underlying transformation in the global corporate culture. It used to be that the sales person was the source of information by which a prospective customer would gain knowledge of new products. The sales person also provided clarity regarding features and benefits, a process by which to purchase and could also sometimes become the account manager for the purchaser.

Now everything is done differently. The client gathers all the information they need from the Internet: specs, comparisons, product and company reviews, and alternate products and suppliers. After the purchase is made multitudes of service people and account managers offer the new customer all levels of support. So where does the sales person fit?

At the same time, while we are struggling to figure out where we fit, we are struggling to stay effective against aggressive negotiating tactics that attack us personally, question our good faith and commitment to the deal and manipulate us toward compromise.

In order to have a true shift in your own way of approaching sales we need to address the very core of the sales process and even more so the core of the sales person.

## DOING OR BELIEVING?

In response to all of this flux and uncertainty, the question we hear most often is, *"Okay, the world is shifting. What do I need to do?"*

Through our experience coaching and managing sales people, we know that this is a trick question. The underlying belief here is that if I follow some basic formula in my actions I will have different results. But life is funny that way – have you ever found that even if you attempt a new technique or try to use a new tool, you still end up with the very same results as before? We assume that what is missing is a prescribed set of action steps that will deliver the results we want. When we don't know what to do, we can just Google it. We can search "How to …" for anything and come up with pages and pages that tell us what to do.

Most people actually know what to do. The greater question is, "What keeps you from doing the things you know you need to do?" We believe the answer to that question lies in another question: What do I need to **believe**?

Deepak Chopra said, "I am not a human thinking, I am not a human doing, I am a human being." When we think that if we simply do the right things, we will have the right results and we will be successful, we are saying, "I am a human doing." *All I have to do is get busy doing.*

Actually, human beings are wired to *do* what we *believe*. We act out of our sense of purpose and what we do is a result of what we believe. If I believe that I can make a sale, I will do all the work that is necessary to make that sale. If I believe that things are going to get difficult, then things are most likely going to get difficult. We become our own self-fulfilling prophecy. We create our way of operating from our way of believing. Mahatma Gandhi described it like this:

Your beliefs become your thoughts,
your thoughts become your words,

your words become your actions,
your actions become your habits,
your habits become your values,
your values become your destiny.

One of the invitations we'd like to make in this book is for you to recognize that what you believe about your context, what you believe about the future, what you believe about selling, all determine how you engage.

If you are afraid, then you are going to act and do things that a fearful person does. If you are hopeful, then you are going to act and do things that a hopeful person does.

So we need to shift our order of operations from believing that if we **do** certain things, we will then be able to **have** the things they want or need, and then we will **be** successful (DO-HAVE-BE). *If I only work harder, then I will have more stuff and I will be happy.* Instead, we need to adopt the order of Be, Do, Have. What we believe about our world and ourselves in the core of our **being**, determines what we will **do**, and ultimately the results we will **have** (BE-DO-HAVE).

The key to transformation lies here.

Now, we are not talking about religious beliefs or moral beliefs. We are talking about things that we believe based on our past experiences that generate a framework or paradigm that either gives us the possibility of thinking something new or staying stuck in the behaviors we have had up until now.

We can teach you new methods and new skills (and we will) but to *do* something different, you first have to *believe* something different; you must explore, develop and adopt new beliefs. Then you can go back to your skill-based learning and you will master the new skills that you would like to engage.

So before we tell you what the sales person should do, let's talk about what we believe and how it either moves us forward or holds us back.

## MOVING FROM POINT A TO POINT B

Our goal in transformation is to move from Point A, our present reality with our current behaviors, to Point B, our desired future with new behaviors.

Too often, though, we get stuck at Point A, trying to fix our current reality. We usually end up frustrated, reacting to our circumstances, managing our current experiences and expectations, without seeing the results we are hoping for.

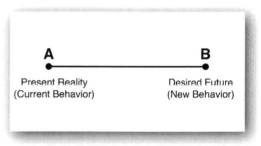

When we're stuck and frustrated, we stop. We disengage and stop participating. Why does this happen? It happens because our limiting beliefs are holding us back.

## LIMITING BELIEFS

A limiting belief is any belief that holds you in your current way of doing things. We all have limiting beliefs, every single one of us. They are internal frames and ways of thinking that keep us from what is possible and what is available out there for us.

Limiting does not necessarily mean that a belief was bad or that it didn't work, or was wrong or untrue. Limiting means it was fixed to a certain frame or to a certain set of variables.

For example, everybody who's been successful in selling has had a winning strategy that has led them to the place where they are right now. That is fantastic. But that winning strategy may not be what is needed for the future. Even though it has been successful, even though it has worked, it is still limited, because it may be irrelevant for the current environment even though it may have been relevant previously.

Or perhaps you have reached a ceiling in your sales performance and you simply have never been able to sell more. What will it take to get you to the next level?

In the future where we are headed the variables have changed. We cannot limit ourselves to the way we thought before, or limit ourselves to the winning strategies that worked in the past. Instead, we get to adopt new strategies; we get to explore new ways of going about things. We get to transform ourselves in order to be relevant for the future.

So, a limiting belief is not always something negative or that has been unsuccessful. A limiting belief is something that may have been relevant in a certain time but in the current context is losing its relevance. It is limited in its capacity to produce results in the future. To uncover our limiting beliefs we have to look at both the things that have been successful for us, and the things that have held us back. And then take a look at what is needed for the future.

The moment we are able to recognize the beliefs that we have had up until now and have carried us to now, we arrive at a place from which we can then develop new beliefs. Those new beliefs will be rooted in curiosity, the willingness to investigate and explore, the willingness to shift and transform, and the willingness to contribute and create value. Once you are able to or willing to engage these new beliefs, you will do new things that will improve your results.

## EXAMPLES OF LIMITING BELIEFS

Our limiting beliefs can roughly be organized into a few broad categories:

**Fear-based beliefs.** These beliefs are rooted in our fears. We might be afraid of hurting people's feelings or damaging a long-term relationship with a client so we are reluctant to have tough conversations. Or we could be afraid of hearing no, so we never ask for the business. These limiting beliefs are generally easier to identify.

**Misguided or false beliefs.** This can be as simple as believing things that are not true, or it can be holding on to "conventional" wisdom without questioning it. For example, it is a common belief that tension in a relationship should be avoided, but tension is actually a vital part of the sales process that you must leverage, and not avoid.

**Misjudgment or overconfidence.** This is when we are disconnected from the reality around us and not reading the situation accurately. We might be under the belief that we are really in control when we are not. Our loyalties can be misplaced and not aligned with our business objectives. We can confuse our business relationships with our personal relationships. We might believe that the way we have always done things is the best way and the only way to be successful.

**Experience-based beliefs.** These are the hardest limiting beliefs to identify and counter because they are often true. Or we at least have experiences that would verify these beliefs. Our competitor has a better product. We know our company has supply constraints and we are not confident we can deliver. We know we do not know all the answers. These things can all be true, but that does not mean we cannot find a way around them.

Here are some more common limiting beliefs in selling. As you read through them we encourage you to write down any of your own limiting beliefs that come to mind.

- *I have to give up on price in order to get the sale.*
- *I will have to make concessions, or add in extras.*
- *I can only speak to a certain level of the organization because I am not qualified.*
- *I am not an expert in risk management or business development for my customer. I am only an expert on our product. Why would they listen to me? I am not running their company.*
- *I am in over my head.*
- *I don't have enough time.*
- *We don't have the resources we need.*
- *I can't get a meeting.*
- *I might make the wrong decision.*
- *My product is irrelevant.*

- *I am afraid of being rejected.*
- *The market has changed too much.*

When we operate from these beliefs, we will prove ourselves right. We are always going to be right about whatever it is we believe. This is the challenge as a human being. We are born lawyers, meaning that if we have a belief about something, we have to have proof that it is correct. So we look for proof all day long. If I think people are unkind, then I will go around the room and I will find evidence all day long to sustain my belief. If, instead, I have a belief that some people are unkind and some people are kind, then I have the openness to see kindness. My paradigm determines my range of operation and belief.

Many successful people and experienced sales professionals have come to a point where they believe that what they believe about the world of sales is the truth, the whole truth, and nothing but the truth. We are suggesting that whatever you know about your sales experience, whatever experience you have had, and whatever success you have had, is limited, because the future includes new variables, new truths, and new opportunities. Innovation and disruptive opportunity will start with saying, *"What if?"*

**What if** I could reach the customer?

**What if** I could break through?

**What if** the customer would buy anyway?

Opportunity is always afforded to the person who recognizes boundaries that exist and decides to go beyond them.

So how do we overcome our fears, uncover the false things we believe, and deal with the things that are true, yet holding us back?

## COUNTERING LIMITING BELIEFS

Overcoming our limiting beliefs requires four simple steps.

1. Recognize and expose the belief.
2. Explore the consequences of holding this belief.
3. Find alternate beliefs.
4. Design new behaviors based on new beliefs.

## 1. RECOGNIZE AND EXPOSE THE BELIEF

The first step to releasing ourselves from a limiting belief is to recognize it and own it. We can only transform what we reveal. We need to articulate the beliefs we are holding and say, "This is a self-limiting belief that has governed or guided me in the past or up until now or at times."

You can use the list above to help you start identifying your own limiting beliefs. While this is a simple process, it is not necessarily an easy one. You may find it helpful to enlist a trusted friend or co-worker as a partner on the journey. A coach would also be especially valuable for guiding you through. At the very least, record your insights in a journal or through some other means.

## 2. EXPLORE THE CONSEQUENCES OF A BELIEF

If you really want to unlock yourself from a limiting belief you have to explore the consequences of that belief. What happens because I am locked to this belief?

The consequence of me believing that the market has closed down is that I don't make phone calls. Or, the consequence of believing my customer is only willing to talk to me about price, not about value, is that I am going to be afraid of talking about value and I am not going to open up the conversation. In fact, I am going to be negotiating with my factory for better pricing.

The consequences of our beliefs are usually revealed in our behavior. If I have a belief that I am not going to be competent enough to talk in a business setting with the CEO, then I am going to avoid phone calls avoid meetings that include senior executives.

If I believe that my product is inferior to my competitor's product, I am most likely going to pitch my product as an inferior product. I am going to act according to my beliefs.

Next, we need to examine the price we are going to pay for our action or inaction based on our limiting belief. It is very important to consider the full sequence of events that will flow out of having a certain belief.

If I believe the market has closed down, I don't make the phone call. If I don't make the phone call, I don't get the meeting. If I don't get the meeting, I don't get the order.

The more honest I am with myself, the more clearly I can realize how much money I am leaving on the table. We think everybody who is reading this book would agree in hindsight that at some point in time they have left money on the table. They left money in a contract because they could have asked for a higher price, they could have asked for a bigger order, or they could have asked for a faster turnaround. But they didn't and they reason they didn't was because at that point in the conversation there was a limiting belief holding them back. They believed that if they did they might lose the contract. They believed that the customer did not have the money.

Hindsight is always 20/20. It is easy to say "If only…" or "I should have done this or said that." Hindsight affords us the opportunity to expose our limiting belief but we cannot stop there. The biggest problem is most people recognize their limiting beliefs and the consequences, but they don't explore alternative beliefs that they could adopt. This is the next step.

## 3. FIND ALTERNATE BELIEFS

We have recognized and explored the consequences of our limiting belief. Now we need to explore **what else is also true**. What other beliefs are available? A limiting belief says this is the only truth that is available. We need to look around for alternate beliefs that we can adopt.

*The market is changing, my product is irrelevant.*

Okay, that might be true. It might **also be true** that there is a new market that your product might be relevant in or there is a new way to position the same product in a different scenario.

*I am going to have to give up on price.*

It could **also be true** that your customer is desperate right now, so though price is important they are anxious to get their product to market.

*Our competitor has a better product.*

It could **also be true** that even though your product doesn't have all the complexity that your competitor's does, your supply chain is much faster than theirs. It could **also be true** that your customer service process is much greater than your competitor's.

What we want to look for are the alternate truths that make new behaviors possible. If it is also true that there are new markets or our customer is desperate or we have better supply chain management or better customer service, then what do we do?

## 4. DESIGN NEW BEHAVIORS

The final step is to outline actions we can take based on our new beliefs or the additional beliefs that are also true. We design our behaviors around our beliefs.

**If this is true, then what?** If our customer service is better, how do we position that or how do we exploit that as an opportunity with our potential customer?

Once we have determined what is also true, then we have to figure out how to go and use it. How do we leverage the alternative belief as a way to engage?

The key is to then sequence our behaviors and identify the first thing that we are going to do. If I believe my product will be relevant to a new market, I will make a plan to reach that new market. If I believe my customer is desperate to get to market, I will map a way forward that will get them the outcomes they need. If I believe that our customer service is better, I will make the phone call to get the meeting. I will move the conversation from price to value and discuss the ways our customer service team can solve the client's challenges.

## WHAT DO YOU BELIEVE?

Remember our chair? We had the choice to change it into a nicer chair or to transform it into a go-kart. Do you want to be a nicer a chair or a go-kart?

Tony Robbins always says, "What do you need to believe in order to get what you want?"

What do you need to believe?

What do you need to stop believing?

Later in this book we are going to show you some of the most important shifts in skill that you will need to make in order to be successful in sales today. But before you can make those shifts in skill and method, you will need to transform your mindset first. We will keep bringing you back to these key questions. In each chapter we are going to ask you to identify the limiting beliefs that will hold you back from making the necessary shift in skill. It all starts with what you believe now, and what you need to believe. Then we can start talking about what you need to do.

Earlier we noted that change often just gives you more of the same thing, while transformation is actually a shift in purpose. The next stop on our journey in transformation is aligning our beliefs with our purpose in selling.

# SHIFTABILITY NOW: CHANGE AND TRANSFORMATION

## KEY TAKEAWAYS

- Change and transformation are not the same thing.
- Transformation is a shift in purpose.
- A limiting belief is any belief that holds you in your current way of doing things.
- Limiting does not necessarily mean that a belief was bad or that it didn't work, or was wrong or untrue. Limiting means it was fixed to a certain frame or to a certain set of variables.
- Overcoming limiting beliefs requires finding new beliefs about what is possible or required for the future.

## SHIFTABILITY MINDSET

1. Identify one or two beliefs you currently hold related to your job or career. How are these beliefs keeping you from moving forward?
2. Are these beliefs fear-based, false, misjudgments or true based on your experience?
3. What are all the consequences of believing this way for you right now? Identify and follow the logical outcome of each consequence.

## SHIFTABILITY ACTION

1. Write out a list of things that are **also true** related to these limiting beliefs.
2. Based on these things that are also true, identify one or two action steps you will now take.

Three

# True North

## NAVIGATING WITH THE COMPASS OF PURPOSE

Efforts and courage are not enough without
purpose and direction.

*John F. Kennedy*

The purpose of life is not to be happy. It is to be
useful, to be honorable, to be compassionate, to
have it make some difference that you have lived
and lived well.

*Ralph Waldo Emerson*

**F**or hundreds of years navigators and lost souls have found their direction using a compass. At its simplest a compass is a floating magnetized needle that aligns itself with the magnetic field of the earth to point north. Once you find north on your compass, and knowing that the sun rises in the east and sets in the west, you can then find the direction you need to go to reach your destination.

As we navigate our way through life and business it is easy to lose our way, especially when the world we have known is in upheaval around us. We need a compass that keeps us aligned with our true north and moving in the right direction. Discovering our purpose and keeping that purpose in our sights will help us navigate. Our purpose is our true north.

## ON PURPOSE

The question of purpose is a very central conversation in business today. Companies are talking about it, managers are wrestling with it, employees are seeking it. But while this is a current discussion, it is certainly not a new one.

Humanity has wrestled with the question of purpose since the dawn of time. Why are we here? What are we supposed to do? We are wired for meaning and driven to find it, not just in our personal lives but also, and perhaps especially in our professional lives or our vocation. Our personal sense of purpose and our professional purpose are inextricably intertwined. However, for the *purposes* of this book we are going to be mainly talking about purpose in the context of your work as a sales professional.

Understanding purpose in the workplace is central to success in selling and a core element of this quality of shiftability that we are exploring. Our work is driven by purpose, defined by purpose and ultimately serves purpose. Our desire for meaning and to serve a greater purpose fuels (energizes) our activity; our understanding of purpose in our context determines how we engage and the moves we make; and ultimately, what we do and how we do it should all aim to serve a purpose. What that purpose actually is will be unique to the context in which you operate.

As a sales professional the context of your purpose is threefold – your individual purpose, the purpose of your role (functional purpose) and the purpose of your organization (corporate purpose). The alignment of these three frames of purpose is where you can make a powerful difference.

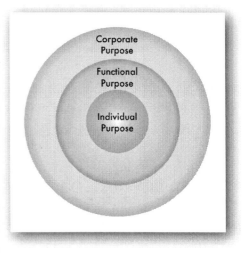

But before we dive into understanding these three frames of purpose we are going to clear up some potential confusion between purpose, vision, mission and values, and take a look at the big picture of purpose and selling.

## THE DIFFERENCE BETWEEN PURPOSE, MISSION, VISION AND VALUES

Sometimes we think we are talking about purpose but we are actually talking about mission or vision or values. These are all very distinct ideas with important but different implications and applications.

### MISSION: WHAT WE DO AND WHO WE DO IT FOR

A mission statement describes the type of work you do, the clients you serve and the level of service you aim to deliver.

**Example:**

"We are in the business of providing world-class logistics software to medium-to-large firms in the manufacturing industry."

### VISION: WHERE ARE WE HEADED?

A vision statement describes where an organization wants to be in some years ahead and sets long-term goals. Vision sets a future context for day-to-day thinking – will the actions we are taking and decisions we are making today move us toward where we want to be? Vision statements are often aspirational: to be the best, to be the leading company, to have our product in every home, etc.

**Example from Amazon:**

"Our vision is to be earth's most customer centric company; to build a place where people can come to find and discover anything they might want to buy online."

## VALUES: HOW WE DO THINGS

Values describe how an organization operates. They set out the desired culture and serve as a compass for conduct.

**Example:**

"We are committed to client satisfaction and serve our clients with care and compassion. We operate according to principles of accountability, sustainability, and responsibility."

## PURPOSE: WHY WE DO WHAT WE DO

Mission explains **what** we do and **whom** we do it for, vision tells us **where** we aim to be, values direct **how** we do it, and purpose tells us **WHY**. Simon Sinek, the author of *Start With Why*, has said, "All the great organizations in the world, all have a sense of why that organization does what it does." Understanding why an organization exists informs everything else. Purpose statements are generally more outward looking and consider the impact an organization or person has on the world round them.

**Example from Apple:**

"To make a contribution to the world by making tools for the mind that advance humankind."

# PURPOSE-DRIVEN SELLING

Selling without a clear purpose is like driving across the continent without a map. It can certainly be done. A lot of people do it. But it is NOT the most effective way to cover the distance and reach your destination. And like that cross-country journey selling takes a lot of support teams to make it happen.

If you start the trip without clearly defining your destination, you can still get somewhere. The question will be – is that where you really want to go? How do you know? How can you tell?

Just "winging it" and "flying by the seat of your pants" in the sales jungle was once the brave thing to do. Now it is just stupid. Now it takes clear understanding about what you are aiming to accomplish, it takes tons of planning and preparation, and it takes diligence in execution. You can no longer serve the needs of today's information-savvy client by just showing up with the latest product brochure in hand. Now you must have a deeper understanding of the customer, their market, their products and their business challenges and the implications of those challenges. And you must start all that with clearly understanding what you are aiming to do from a higher-level perspective of purpose.

And while the noble cause of making a profit may in fact be a fine goal, in this case it does not qualify as a **purpose**.

A company's core purpose, as defined in *Built to Last* by Jim Collins and Jerry Porras, is "the organization's fundamental reason for being. An effective purpose reflects the importance people attach to the company's work – it taps their idealistic motivation -- and gets at the deeper reasons for an organization's existence beyond just making money."

From both a corporate and a personal perspective, we like the simplification of this idea that Roy M. Spence and Haley Rushing have in their book *It's Not What You Sell, It's What You Stand For*. In their book they give the following as their simplest way to explain purpose: "Purpose is a definitive statement about the difference you are trying to make in the world".

Both books clearly show that purpose-driven organizations are amongst the most successful in the world, and that leaders who clearly understand the power of purpose drive these organizations.

Understanding and having a clear purpose may not be the answer to everything needed to be successful. Without it, however, the battle to succeed is made more complex and many times more likely to be lost. The choice is yours. Lead and sell from a clear purpose – or not.

Selling with purpose, or purpose-driven selling, is about creating value for people through understanding what they need as an individual in their corporate role, and then providing solutions. This requires understanding your own individual purpose and your functional purpose for why you sell and understanding the corporate purpose for what your company stands for, not just what it sells. All wrapped together, purpose-driven selling provides a unique client engagement level that everyone, client included, values more.

When we start talking about purpose, the term "selling" can be understood in a different way. When you are fully engaged in purpose-driven selling you are not actually selling. You are helping someone buy, or acquire, whatever it is that they need to fulfill their purpose at that time. Again, a subtle shift in thinking makes a big change in how we communicate and how we engage with clients. Selling is simply a transaction that enables purpose – your client's purpose, your company's purpose and your purpose.

## UNDERSTANDING MY PURPOSE AS AN INDIVIDUAL

Mark Twain said, "The two most important days in your life are the day you are born and the day you find out why."

Wondering why we are here is fundamental to the human condition. It's a profound moment when we start to catch a glimpse of just what our purpose might be. This discovery is the starting point of living an intentional life aligned to your purpose.

Many authors wiser than we are have written extensively on the notion of personal purpose and living a purposeful life. There's a lot to be said – more than we will attempt to cover here. But there are a few points we would like to make.

As a sales professional your sense of individual purpose is central to your success and effectiveness. If you don't have an understanding of your own purpose, you need to take the time to identify and define it for yourself. Understanding your purpose is not just a process of discovery and recognition; it's also a process of declaration and decision.

For some there is an obvious natural gifting and calling to be stepped into. For the rest of us, purpose is more about choices and determining how we want our story to play out. Napoleon Hill, author of *Think and Grow Rich* wrote, "What a different story men would have to tell if only they would adopt a definite purpose and stand by that purpose until it had time to become an all-consuming obsession!"

We like this simple diagram that illustrates how the different spheres of your existence overlap and intersect. In this perspective, your purpose is found at the intersection of your passion, mission, profession and vocation.

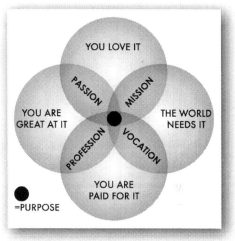

These are some common elements of individual purpose:

- Fulfilling work (and the greatest fulfillment often comes from serving)
- Providing for self/family
- Learning and growing
- Reaching personal potential
- Leaving a legacy
- Making a difference

This last point brings us back to Spence and Rushing's definition of purpose being a statement made about the "difference we are trying to make in the world."

Jackie Robinson said, "A life is not important except in the impact it has on other lives."

**What kind of difference do you want to make?** This is a question you should ask both personally and professionally – because you *can* make a difference as a sales professional.

## UNDERSTANDING THE PURPOSE OF MY ROLE

William Damon, Director of Stanford University's Center on Adolescence and leading scholar of human development, defines purpose as "a stable and generalized intention to accomplish something that is at once meaningful to the self and **of consequence to the world beyond the self.**"

Moving out from purpose at more of an existential level, we come to the purpose of the role you are in. You likely have more than one role. You may be an applications engineer or sales person but likely you are also a parent or a spouse or a mentor or caregiver and so on. Your purpose is of consequence beyond yourself.

The nature of functional purpose is often more concrete and more easily defined than our existential purpose. You can start with your job description. Why were you hired? What expectations do you need to meet?

Here are some elements of purpose in a sales professional role:

- To get the right products to the people who need them
- To help clients discover opportunities to improve
- To help clients solve problems
- To create value
- To deliver insight
- To provide solutions
- To help your company meet its purpose
- To help your client meet their purpose

This is perhaps the most important question to ask: How can you help both your clients **and** your company serve their purpose?

## UNDERSTANDING CORPORATE PURPOSE

Nikos Mourkogiannis argues in his book *Purpose: The Starting Point of Great Companies* that purpose is crucial to a firm's success: it is the primary source of achievement and reveals the underlying human dynamics of any human activity:

"Purpose is crucial for all truly successful enterprises. Let others play with 'strategy' and 'tactics' and 'management'. Purpose is the game of champions. Only strong-minded men and women – adults with powerful intellects and real character and spines of steel – are suited for it...Purpose is bigger than ambition or greed. Purpose is bigger than strategy. Enron had strategy – indeed it had many strategies. But strategies are about means; they cannot be an end in themselves. An end is a reason. Enron lacked a reason – it lacked Purpose."

For a company to truly make a difference over a long period of time it must have clear directions by which it makes decisions and views its challenges. Good times and bad times are best guided by clear understanding of both the company's values and its true purpose. A purpose that is BIGGER than revenue, bigger than profits, bigger than return on working capital and all the other very key metrics of corporate financial success.

However, profits are key to the life of the corporation. One of the Value Statements at Mitch's company is "Profits provide for everything we do." If you do not maintain a steadfast focus on creating and delivering profits, whether you are a public company or a privately owned company, the value that you deliver to your clients will simply not survive.

But profits are the outcome of actions, not the driving force. Purpose is built on a higher plane than profitability and it feeds that never-ending hunger for more profits. Defining and focusing on purpose is actually highly profitable.

A truly effective corporate purpose statement should compel the soul to action. It should emotionally touch the humanity in each person such that we clearly know why we are working hard on the behalf of others.

We highlighted Apple's corporate purpose statement above. Here are some more examples from other companies:

ING's purpose is **"Empowering people to stay a step ahead in life and in business"**.
The Kellogg food company's purpose is **"Nourishing families so they can flourish and thrive"**.
The insurance company IAG purpose statement says, **"We help make your world a safer place"**.

All of these statements appeal to our humanity. "Nourishing thriving families" is far more inspirational than *increasing our share of the breakfast cereal market* would be. And "making the world a safer place" is a far more noble purpose than *selling more insurance.*

What is the corporate purpose you are working towards?

## UNDERSTANDING THE PURPOSE OF THE CLIENT

When you have aligned your understanding of your purpose as a sales professional with the corporate purpose of your company, with your individual purpose at the core, it is easy to make the leap to understanding your client's purpose – because they are operating in the same threefold context.

You are working with individuals who are trying, just like you, to align and serve their individual purpose with the purpose of their role and the purpose of their company.

The opportunity is for you to start with understanding their purpose in all its dimensions both personal and professional, and then work to provide insight and solutions that will serve all facets. Here is one example of what that looks like in action.

In Mitch's company, one of the Field Apps Engineers had been working with an industrial control company in the Midwest U.S. They had done many projects with the design teams over the years and another large project was coming up for a sourcing decision. Mitch's team did all of the technical and systems analysis and worked hard to understand the business issues that were being faced. The team proposed a solid answer that delivered on solving the business issues and handled all of the technical needs. They won that project.

Following up with the client's engineering team some time later, Mitch discovered the REAL reason they had won. It seems that the head engineer had a young son and he was coaching that young son's little league team that summer. Experience with Microchip had shown that engineer that their resources and team could be counted on to help keep the project rolling smoothly which meant that he could easily leave work at 4:30 on those two days each week that his son's team had practice. The personal win was the difference maker. We will come back to another story a lot like this in a later chapter and see how understanding and operating from purpose deeply influences your ability to deliver personalized insight.

## LIVING AND WORKING ON PURPOSE

Understanding and embracing our purpose will energize and direct everything we do.

Keeping anchored in your purpose is going to be essential to your success in implementing the skills we are going to talk about. It is going to help you overcome fears and obstacles, give you the courage to try new things, and keep you going when things get tough.

Our purpose lies at the heart of what motivates us.

When you ask sales people why they have chosen this profession you will likely get a wide variety of answers. Almost always when you dig deep it is not the love of competing or greed for money that is the most compelling factor. What truly comes out is the higher-level simple love of helping people. All of the other motivations are in play, but the really big tug is the desire to help people in some way. This really does point to having a purpose and pursuing it.

Operating from a sense of purpose does require a shift in understanding. Understanding why you really do what you do, not just for income. We need to understand why the companies that we work for truly exist and the higher purpose they serve. And then seek understanding about your client's purpose. You may even end up shifting how they think about themselves and help them see the greater purpose that they serve.

# SHIFTABILITY NOW: UNDERSTANDING OUR PURPOSE

## KEY TAKEAWAYS

- Our work is driven by purpose, defined by purpose and ultimately serves purpose.
- Mission explains **what** we do and **whom** we do it for, vision tells us **where** we aim to be, values direct **how** we do it, and purpose tells us **WHY**.
- We need to understand our individual purpose, the purpose of the role we are in, and the corporate purpose of the company we work for.
- Your clients are trying, just like you, to align and serve their individual purpose with the purpose of their role and the purpose of their company.
- Understanding and embracing our purpose will energize and direct everything we do.

## SHIFTABILITY MINDSET

1. What do you believe about your purpose as an individual?
2. What do you believe about your purpose as a sales professional? What do you **need** to believe?
3. What is your company's purpose? If there isn't an existing stated purpose, what do you think it is?

## SHIFTABILITY ACTION

1. Write out a personal purpose statement. You may find it helpful to write about your mission (what you do and who you do it for), vision (where you are headed) and values (how you operate) to lead you to clarifying your purpose.
2. Write out what you know about the purposes of one of your clients: individual, role and corporate. Aim to discover more about their purpose: ask questions, do some research.

Part 2

# Shifting Our Skillset

Skillset is both *what* you do and *how* you do it. They say the longest journey is the twelve inches from your head to your heart, or the other way from the heart to the head. It is certainly challenging to shift our beliefs and our thinking. The hard work of exploring limiting beliefs or stuck thinking can feel overwhelming at times, and yet once we have started to shift our beliefs and our thinking another great task awaits us –moving from our heart and head to our hands.

This journey to hand can be as long or even longer. Practicing our new learning. Expressing our new found shiftability in mindset in a creative and value generating way. Believing is not enough. It is said that even the Devil believes – what you *DO* is ultimately the sign of generating a congruent frame. In this next part we will explore skills that are authentic reflections of a shiftable mindset.

Four

# Be Like Water

## SHIFTABILITY #1: MASTERING AND APPLYING DIFFERENT STYLES OF SALES ENGAGEMENT

An effective and relevant sales professional is nimble and can apply different styles of sales engagement to different situations.

Be like water.

*Bruce Lee*

You can get everything in life you want if you will just help enough other people get what they want.

*Zig Ziglar, Secrets of Closing the Sale*

B ruce Lee, one of the most influential martial artists of all time, initially trained as a young man in the tradition of Wing Chun. Later in life he developed his own integrated martial arts philosophy in contrast to the rigid and formalistic disciplines of traditional martial arts. His new system, *Jeet Kune Do,* instead emphasized practicality, flexibility, speed and efficiency. Lee adapted techniques and training methods from different martial arts systems as well as fencing and boxing. In his own words, *Jeet Kune Do* "utilizes all ways and is bound by none and, likewise, uses any techniques which serve its end."

In one of his most famous quotes, Lee described what flexibility in form looks like:

> Don't get set into one form, adapt it and build your own, and let it grow, be like water. Empty your mind; be formless, shapeless — like water. Now you put water in a cup, it becomes the cup; you put water into a bottle it becomes the bottle; you put it in a teapot it becomes the teapot. Now water can flow or it can crash. Be water, my friend.

Just like the traditional martial arts masters of old, there are plenty of people out there who will tell you that there is only one right way to sell. Today they will tell you that solution selling is dead, or that relationship builders are ineffective in today's economy, or that whatever sales practices you have used in the past are now irrelevant. These same people will likely tell you that you now need to adopt a singular, new methodology.

We disagree. Like Bruce Lee, we believe that you need to be like water. You need to adopt principles of practicality and flexibility, and use all while being bound by none. This is the first principle in applying the shiftability mindset to developing the shiftability skillset in sales.

All things have their place and time and this goes for sales methodologies as well. There is no such thing as one singular right way to do things. Any successful sales method or style of engagement depends first on understanding clearly what the client needs to do in one of three areas: grow revenue, reduce costs, or mitigate risk. This requires an understanding of purpose – your client's corporate purpose and their individual purpose. This is a complex undertaking, which is good, and makes it defensible and removes it from the commodity status.

This understanding must take place in a multidimensional matrix. First, you need to understand your client's needs and challenges, and frame conversations based on their role, their position in their company, their position in their decision-making process, and where they are in their own stage of the decision-making process. Based on this understanding, you then need to apply an appropriate situational client engagement style.

This is the first shiftability skill for staying relevant and effective in selling today:

**There are different styles of client engagement, needed at different times, with different people and different roles, and you will need to master shifting from one engagement style to another, as appropriate.**

## FOUR STYLES OF CLIENT ENGAGEMENT

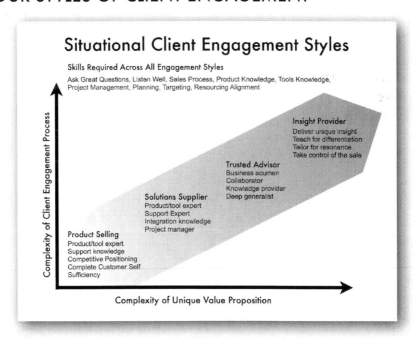

Broadly speaking there are four main styles of client engagement, moving from simpler engagement to more complex interactions. You can move through the styles sequentially with a particular client or you may find yourself totally stuck in the lowest level possible with some of those same people and clients. In many cases, the style of engagement will be dictated by the role of the people that you interface with inside of the client. The larger the client, the more vertical an organization, the narrower a person's role will likely become.

While the higher levels of engagement are more optimal for differentiating and creating unique value, it's important to understand that the reality of selling may in fact have us acting in all four styles with any one client at any one time. As professionals in this space we need to clearly know when to adopt what style and be able to move from style to style, even within a single conversation.

The four main styles are:

- Product Selling
- Solutions Supplier
- Trusted Advisor
- Insight Provider

## PRODUCT SELLING

The most basic level of engagement is when your role is limited to offering up simple product answers to basic product requests. As an example, in semiconductor sales, sales people call on individuals who are part of companies that are designing and manufacturing electronic products. They call on purchasing and engineering teams and they feel valuable when they provide technology assistance, data, and competitive comparisons when asked to do so by the people that they work with inside of the client. While it feels good to service these requests quickly, accurately, and as requested, the truth is that there is virtually no value added by the individual serving at this level. A lifetime spent in this mode will most certainly be extremely stressful, as your entire competitive framework will be built around one thing only - offering the lowest possible price. Forever!

This is the sales role that we are most familiar with and it is the engagement style that, for the most part, worked in the early years of the B2B selling model. It just does not work now. This old world role is sadly the role in which many sales people today still reside. And even more sadly, most of the sales teams operating in this mode around the world find themselves backed into the corner where their only out is to battle in the Product Seller price match. While most sales professionals know that the disintermediation of the Internet on its own has made this style totally obsolete, their own leadership and upper management teams are still stuck in the past, afraid to escape the gravitational pull of doing what they have always done.

## SOLUTIONS SUPPLIERS

The next rung on the ladder is Solutions Supplier. It is a step up from the Product Seller, and that is good. As we become Solutions Suppliers it requires more knowledge of the ecosystem within our own company and how to help a client get the most assistance from us in completing their product development. Project management is a skill set needed here.

However, solution selling still does not offer significant opportunity for differentiation, and is often simply grouping product selling into a system-level offering. It assumes that as the seller, you know more about the end user's true needs than they may know themselves, and you can provide them with a combination of products that solve their challenges.

While that on occasion may actually be true, the hard, cold fact is that this level of engagement is just as quickly commoditized as the Product Seller and actually limits true innovation. Solution Suppliers have evolved along a path that often times has them offering up their own version of reference designs of complete products or complete functions inside of products. An example of this would be a supplier that offers up the total portion of the control electronics needed to operate a washing machine motor to a company that builds washing machines. Once upon a time many clients were willing to take these reference designs and simply build them as offered up and include them in their products. That led to little differentiation in end products and a spread of commoditization. Instead, now a "proof of concept" may be offered up that is specific to the client and their unique needs. Now, we have customized Solutions Suppliers in a race to commoditize their customization efforts in addition to their own products.

Climbing to the lofty levels of the next two rungs on the ladder to become Trusted Advisors or Insight Providers requires significant time invested in learning and understanding the specifics of the client's own business and the needs of *their* clients. Here you step out of your own skin totally and learn to walk in their shoes. It requires significant business acumen and huge amounts of empathy. To us the greatest trait needed to master these two levels is curiosity. Your curiosity must be based on a sincere desire to help your clients make a difference.

## TRUSTED ADVISORS AND INSIGHT PROVIDERS

When we move up to Trusted Advisor we are now in the position where a client seeks us out for input and ideas to help them solve business problems they are facing. Many times this level of engagement has us working with a client in areas well beyond our own product or solution offerings.

The most complex style is that of the Insight Provider. Here we work closely with a client and help them see things in a different light than they have. We take control of our engagement by guiding the conversations in the right direction. Our biggest help to a client here is helping them THINK DIFFERENTLY than they have in the past. Our work requires a solid understanding of how our products and solutions can best help them create value that they do not see today. While we guide, consult, think, and teach, it is done with an outcome in mind that works toward a solution that we can provide, not just giving away free consulting.

There are subtle differences between a Trusted Advisor and an Insight Provider. Both require that you truly have your client's trust and that is a neutral position from which you work to their benefit. As a true Trusted Advisor the client will reach out and call on you to help them with matters that are not even related to the products or services that you provide. They count on you knowing their world very well and that you are open enough to serve them without bias. And that's tough. Being a Trusted Advisor may start off more as a responsive role.

In contrast, the shift into Insight Provider is more proactive, requiring significant research and preparation work before you offer up what you have created that will impact them so positively. It takes preparation to understand, create, and then deliver the first insight offering, which will in fact just be the start of the more powerful discovery and co-creation of insight done in collaboration with your client.

## SITUATIONAL CLIENT ENGAGEMENT IN ACTION

Mitch's team works with a very large manufacturer of data communication products. Let's see how the various styles play out within this one client. The relationship started out as simply fulfilling a request for data on a product beyond what had been published on the company website. The team worked with both engineering and purchasing in the **Product Seller** style for some time until they could build a case for the evolution of our discussions.

From that point they moved to **Solutions Supplier**, providing more data and information on a higher level of engineering work, delivering complete function-level data that was beyond the scope of published data on the web site. Through doing this very well and offering up much more than the client ever requested, over time the team's relationship with the client has evolved such that they now call to talk about issues above and beyond what they actually offer.

Mitch's team has now risen to the ranks of **Trusted Advisor** within the higher levels of the client. Recently, their understanding of the client's business has allowed them to offer some significant insights, which will help the client develop their products faster and get to market much more efficiently than they have in the past. The **Insight Provider** level of discussion happens mostly at a higher operational level before sharing it more broadly around the organization. When you develop insight in a co-creation mode with a client, they will champion these ideas as their own and will begin sharing them within their own walls.

We will be learning more about providing insight and other skills that are useful for navigating these higher-level relationships in upcoming chapters. But first, you must anchor the application of these skills in a solid understanding of your client and their needs.

## UNDERSTANDING THE CLIENT

As Trusted Advisors and Insight Providers, we must build our conversations in such a way that adds value based upon *whom* we are communicating with and *what* they value in their world. This comes from preparation. It means having a solid understanding of the technical needs and the business issues that each client faces and then proactively addressing all of those challenges at every level of a client.

The ultimate aim is to develop and deliver personalized insight that **co-creates** client value (more on this soon.) You will create this with the very client-specific perspective that comes from an intersection of understanding the role of the person you are working with, where they are in the client decision making process, and what type of engagement you are working on at just that moment.

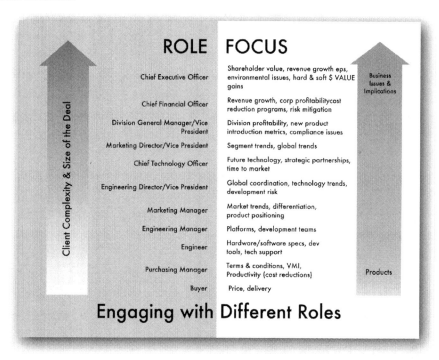

To be an expert in client engagement requires carefully listening and learning, and looking to understand their purpose so that we can work with it.

Underpinning all the styles of client engagement is skilled relationship building, which is really about the art of connection.

## CREATING CONNECTION

Effective client engagement depends on a high degree of connection between you and the client. The objective evolves from forming and sustaining the relationship to *transforming* the relationship and increasing the zone of potential and agreement.

Connection is the place where you have gained trust and permission with an individual or group. It is the process whereby you and the buyer have "clicked".

Creating connection is about mutuality and is a process of discovering and creating agreement on shared paradigms and points of reference.

Some people are naturally good at creating connection when first meeting someone. Others need to work a little harder at it, but it is a skill that one can develop. When we first meet people and engage in small talk, we usually start with looking for a common memory connection. We look for points of mutual interest or experience like football for example, or a TV show or perhaps a school or university. This memory connection explores the possibility that somewhere we have a shared experience. Once we have established a frame for our memory search (last week's game or event) we move to the next level of singling out a memory that we are looking to explore and find out if in fact we do have a shared experience.

This sounds something like this:

*"Did you watch the game on Sunday?"* (Scary waiting period to see if the connection context will work.)

*"Sure did!"* (Yes! There is potential and we can now explore the memory bank for a shared experience, opinion or frame.)

*"Can you believe the call on #10 in the last minute?"*

*"Unbelievable - that was outrageous!"* (YEEHAW! We have a shared experience from which we can now generate a greater connection.)

When we share a collective memory it leads to affinity trust. Affinity trust implies that we have made a number of memory connections; it says that we have points of view that are congruent *and that our minds have collided into basic agreement.*

Uncovering mutuality figuratively resets the seating at a meeting. We move emotionally from opposite sides of the table to sitting next to each other looking at the same screen of memories. This repositioning allows us to dissolve barriers of disconnection and will rapidly build the premise for potential agreement. Sometimes it may even be a good idea to change your physical position to actually sitting next to each other, if possible.

## CONNECTION AND CURIOSITY

We are more likely to create connection when we are curious. Curiosity is different from being investigative. Curiosity is the desire to learn, to discover. It recognizes that we don't know what we don't know.

In contrast, being investigative is looking for evidence to prove that what we have thought all along is so. We look to confirm what we believe we already know and to prove that we are right. It is a very different experience for your client when you are wanting to learn versus when you are wanting to be right.

In our coaching experience, we have seen that this tension of wanting to be right can be particularly challenging for sales engineers (also called applications engineers or field application engineers). Engineers are often right. In fact, being right is an important value for them – their research, documents and analytics are core to their value proposition. However, sales engineers can tend to overlook **context.** Context is not about the facts or "what is there", but rather about how what is there *occurs* for the client. Context is the client's relationship to the facts and information. You can have all the facts right but if you get the context wrong, you will lose the client.

However, if you approach the situation with the curiosity to discover and understand your client's context you will be better able to create connection. This curiosity allows you to discover the client's paradigm, point of view and the way they experience their context.

People don't engage based on facts. People engage based on the way they relate to their context.

Curiosity allows us to create a larger area for agreement. Fact-finding is about checking boxes. Curiosity is about widening the playing field. Of course, key in the process of curiosity is ensuring that what we are hearing is actually what the client is saying.

**People can't hear what you are saying while they are busy listening to what they are thinking.**

We have often worked with sales leaders using the statement above as an anchor thought. Perhaps you have been in that conversation before. You are talking and then you can see at about ten seconds into sharing your counterpart's eyes have glossed over and you know that while you are spilling your guts they are no longer present. The lights are on, but nobody is home. You can see that their mind is busy elsewhere; their gaze has moved from being locked on to your eyes to looking at your mouth, waiting for signs that you are no longer talking so they can say what is on their mind.

Perhaps you too have been that person – not listening to your client but thinking of your response and how you are going to stun them with your brilliance once you get the floor back. Don't be that person. We often lose our clients, not because we can't talk, but because we are not present when we should be listening.

Being **present** while you are being **curious** will elevate your connection exponentially.

## I HEAR YOU

The next part of creating connection is acknowledgement. When people feel like they are being seen and heard, it moves the connection to a whole new level. While curiosity ensures that you will discover the client's point of view and context, acknowledgement recognizes the crucial role the client plays in their context.

In acknowledging the client, not only are you establishing mutuality, you are also affirming the person. Your client feels recognized and perhaps even valued as part of the conversation. Acknowledgement personalizes the process and the decision maker is affirmed as integral to the process.

Acknowledgement is an emotional anchor and will build the emotional equity that we are looking for. This equity will grow even more if we share of ourselves. Vulnerability leads to amazing connection. Vulnerability does not equal weakness. In fact, vulnerability is an invitation to mutual sharing.

In the early days of Hendre's facilitator training for large group awareness programs, a mentor told the trainees that a good introduction always includes "telling on yourself." Telling on yourself is sharing from your own weakness in order to give the people in the room permission to be honest and truthful about their own state. When we are willing to be vulnerable like this we are actually creating permission for the client to do the same. We move to sharing and collaborating instead of trying to outmaneuver each other.

## WALKING WITH KINGS AND COMMONERS

Mastering the art of shifting your style of engagement as the context demands requires being willing to adapt your way of relating to your client. You must be willing to adapt in order to connect in a way that allows for the greatest possibility of success.

Rudyard Kipling wrote this in his wonderful poem *If*:

*If you can talk with crowds and keep your virtue,*
*Or walk with Kings—nor lose the common touch,*
*If neither foes nor loving friends can hurt you,*
*If all men count with you, but none too much;*

Too often, we want to impress people with being intelligent, having all the answers or perhaps looking successful by the car we drive, the watch on our wrist and the clothes we wear. Being "impressive" sometimes has the opposite effect of what we are really looking for. When people are impressed they may actually be intimidated, or there may even be a chance that they while like your clothes, watch and resume, they don't really like you.

Hendre has had the privilege of coaching and training professionals all over the world, and has spent a lot of time working in Brazil over the last ten years. This country is complex and filled with potential and possibility. It also has, like any other country, its fair share of corruption and systemic class discrimination. After most workshops they have time for open floor feedback and more than once Hendre has heard people say, "Hendre, you are such a simple man and yet you share some good wisdom."

When you hear that comment out of context it may sound a bit offensive. When we grew up, being "simple" meant not being sophisticated or not having broad experiences, or maybe not even being very intelligent. But in the context of these workshops Hendre has made a conscious decision to not oversell his experience or share much about his success, but rather to be kind and truly caring about the success of his participants.

Rudyard Kipling's version of being simple does not equal not having sophistication; it means that *your sophistication does not have you*. The simplicity of shiftability is being able to adapt to the context in a way that creates value for the client without compromising your own values. Kipling invites us to consider that our identity is not derived from whom we are with, but rather *how* we are with people regardless of who they are.

In the world of selling, this means that we are as comfortable (and kind) with the procurement assistant as we are with the CEO. Having a simple commitment to connecting with your client will allow you to be adaptable.

It is funny how flexibility allows for greater possibility. We often confuse flexibility with compromise. We wrongly believe that if we are flexible, it means that we must be willing to compromise our values or that flexibility may include giving up margin in a particular deal. This is not what we mean here. Shiftability allows you to maintain values, and possibly even increase margins, while being able to change your posture or the way you initially related to the possibility.

So be like water: be curious, connect, create value, increase the possibility and get the business.

# SHIFTABILITY NOW: MASTERING CLIENT ENGAGEMENT

## KEY TAKEAWAYS

- I need to master different styles of engagement and be flexible in applying them.
- There is a place and need for every style of engagement.
- Higher levels of engagement offer more opportunity for differentiation and creating real value.
- Creating connection is vital for all styles and levels of engagement. Connection depends on mutuality, curiosity and affirmation.

## SHIFTABILITY MINDSET

1. What limiting beliefs are holding me back from engaging with my clients at a higher level? (Remember limiting beliefs may be false or they may be true. Ask yourself, what else is true?)
2. Can you identify different levels in your current client engagement? Are you stuck at being a Product Seller or Solutions Provider?

## SHIFTABILITY ACTION

1. List three things you can do now to create greater connection with a specific client. Write down when you will put these into action.
2. Target the specific level of engagement you would like to move to with this client. What will you do towards that goal?

Five

# It's Complicated

## SHIFTABILITY #2: EMBRACING COMPLEXITY
An effective and relevant sales professional knows there is opportunity in complexity and can navigate through it with simple communication.

> The complexity that we despise is the complexity that leads to difficulty. It isn't the complexity that raises problems. There is a lot of complexity in the world. The world is complex. That complexity is beautiful. I love trying to understand how things work. But that's because there's something to be learned from mastering that complexity.
>
> WARD CUNNINGHAM, INVENTOR OF THE WIKI

**T**he ostrich is native to the savannahs of Africa and is the largest species of bird, weighing in at 350 pounds. It is also the fastest mammal on two legs. And, as everyone knows, when an ostrich senses danger or sees a predator it will bury its head in the sand, thinking that if it can't see the predator, the predator can't see it. Of course, this is the origin of the common idiom *to bury your head in the sand.*

Except it's not true.

An ostrich actually does what any sensible creature does in the face of danger: it runs away and it runs away quickly. The myth about ostriches burying their heads in the sand probably originated from observations of them with their heads down tending their nests or eating pebbles and sand to aid with digestion. But it is a myth that endures and is widely believed by most people.

Here is another myth that many believe: **simplicity is always best and complexity is bad.**

Complexity makes us nervous, overwhelms us and even scares us because we don't know what to do with it. Our instinct is to seek simplicity and avoid complexity by desperately trying to reduce complex situations to simple variables.

So when we are confronted with complicated situations, like the mythical ostrich or the real ostrich, we bury our heads in the sand and hope it will go away, or we run in the other direction as fast as our two legs can carry us.

In the world of complex B2B sales, the reality is that complexity is actually our friend. If we shift away from favoring simplicity and instead choose to embrace complexity and look it square in the eye, we will be able to open up so much more opportunity to create value with and for our clients. Because, here's the thing – your client is probably running away from complexity, too.

## COMPLEXITY IS OUR FRIEND

In a simple sale, there is little differentiation and everything usually comes down to a simple proposition of price. This is a basic scenario with limited opportunity to influence or add value. But a salesperson that can take that simple proposition of price alone and open it back up to exploring more complex underlying fundamentals will be able to create more opportunity and more value. And, in a complicated sale, with multiple variables and challenges that demand a complex solution, most clients will welcome the help of a skilled navigator.

Complexity really is our friend.

How can this be true? Everyone knows that a salesperson's best ammunition is the simple list of silver bullet product features and benefits. It is also known that the very best things to have are perfect products that literally sell themselves, right? Sounds right, should be right. Nice and simple. So how can complexity be our friend?

Keeping things simple used to work, but it doesn't work anymore. As we just noted, the simpler the answer to a need, the less differentiated it will be, and the only competitive position will come down to price. Price wars do not need sales people to be involved because machines can take care of all of that. When all that matters is price, then sales people don't matter. We simply don't have much to offer in that situation.

So, what do you do when you find yourself caught in a simple price-only situation?

You ratchet back up the **complexity** of the entire client interaction. You can take a simple proposition (price alone) and open it back up to explore the fundamentals leading to the decision based on price alone.

To do this you go back to the beginning where it all started, when that first product pitch was made, and shift everything.

This goes to the heart of the client engagement process and everything we discussed in the previous chapter about being able to master different styles of client engagement. A simple sale is most likely taking place in the lower levels of engagement as Product Sellers and Solution Suppliers. Engaging as Trusted Advisors and Insight Providers where there is more opportunity for greater success, is inherently more complex.

Embracing complexity requires us to dig very deeply into every motivation and understanding what the client needs to fix, accomplish, or avoid. To eventually provide the best solution possible to the client we need to get a grasp of every business issue, every organizational issue, and every personal issue, and jointly develop ideas and action plans to handle every single one of them. If we are going to differentiate our offering, we must differentiate what we do. This level of human understanding requires a great deal of caring and is anchored back in our understanding of purpose. If we are to engage and deliver the deepest level of response that we possibly can, we need to understand and diagnose at the highest possible level with hundreds of great two-way conversations at the heart of the creation. You have to want to help from your heart and it needs to show. In this case, you can't fake it till you make it - the client will know.

Navigating complexity starts with preparation and research. It means we need to spend as much time as possible in the shoes of the people that we are serving. Public companies tell the world everything we need to know. We just need to look into published corporate filings to know what their concerns and risks are at a corporate level. We will learn the competitive nature of their business and the structure of their company.

Understanding and responding to risks is often of more value to most companies than driving revenue. It represents an area where very few resources from the outside are helping them. You can differentiate more in helping a client manage risk than any other element. Managing risk also involves a more complete understanding of the client and your own offering and resources. Operating at this higher level is a key differentiating and competitive factor in your favor.

It is important to note that finding and using the complexity in a sales situation is not about obfuscation or confusing your client with smoke and mirrors. Misunderstanding this principle could tempt you into layering a veneer of complexity and complicating things with incomprehensible jargon and impenetrable solutions that overwhelm your client so that they throw their hands up in frustration and just let you run with it because they can't understand it.

Complex problems often require complex solutions, but that does not mean that they can't be communicated simply with clear and easy to understand education and guidance. In fact, simple communication is vital. Einstein said, "If you can't explain it simply, you don't understand it well enough."

# NAVIGATING COMPLEX NEEDS WITH SIMPLE COMMUNICATION

So, we've established that delivering a complex solution that addresses complex client needs makes your offering more defensible and more valuable than a typical competitive-product-only response.

The next challenge is making the complex simple to understand for your client, which is really an art form. Leading a client through complex needs and solutions requires simple navigation, communication and direction. The aim is to help the client discover their actual needs, understand true value propositions, and see the path to the solution.

Our fear of complexity arises out of how we relate to the situation – we get overwhelmed. You have probably heard this question: How do you eat an elephant? One bite at a time. And this famous aphorism: "The journey of a thousand miles starts with one step." In complex sales, one of your most important roles is as navigator, guiding your client step-by-step, one bite at a time.

Here are some simple principles for navigating complex needs and solutions.

## LET EVERYTHING ELSE BE SIMPLE.

This refers to everything around the sale: schedules, phone calls, meetings, communication, and people involved. Streamline the team, schedule fewer meetings, keep emails short, and keep communication precise. Remove clutter and unnecessary complications.

## BREAK IT DOWN.

This is the simple art of breaking apart the pieces into the smallest, easy to understand chunks. Then handle each small part on its own, with its own unique response. From there, you can take the smaller parts and start building a bigger picture together. It's like a jigsaw puzzle with a thousand small pieces making the big picture. Only in this case, you do not have a finished picture on the box guiding your thinking. You have to build and develop it as you go.

## AVOID JARGON AND COMPLICATED LANGUAGE.

Throwing out acronyms or highly technical terms and industry in-speak may make you feel smarter, but really it just makes everyone else feel a little bit dumb and makes you less likable. Always ask yourself if there is a better way to say something. Put yourself in your client's shoes – do they have the context to understand what you are saying? What do they need to know first? How can you explain it better?

We are not suggesting that you "dumb" things down. Simple communication actually requires far greater sophistication and effort. And we definitely don't want you to be patronizing or condescending. Working through complexity with your client requires respectful collaboration.

It may seem that we are contradicting ourselves here, saying that the greatest opportunity is in complexity and then telling you to simplify things. There is a principle in philosophy called Occam's Razor. Roughly, the premise is that **more things should not be used than are necessary**. It has also been stated this way: **usually the simplest answer is the right one**.

For example, if you wake up to discover that a tree has fallen in your front yard, you could form a couple of hypotheses about what happened: 1. It was a windy night and the tree blew down: 2. A drunk driver came through your neighborhood, was blinded by an oncoming car, drove into the tree and knocked it down, and then drove away. Obviously, the simple answer that the wind blew it down is the most likely explanation.

But don't overlook this key word in the premise: **necessary**. Maintaining this paradoxical balance between complexity and simplicity hinges on identifying and understanding what is necessary. A complex solution with many parts may be necessary; confusing, complicated communication is not necessary.

Another saying attributed to Einstein sums it up well: **Everything should be made as simple as possible, but not simpler.**

## A POWERFUL QUESTION: WHAT ELSE?

We are continually rediscovering how complex situations hold more opportunity. Just one example is an industrial control client that Mitch's team was developing. They designed and built commercial heating and cooling systems for small to medium-sized commercial buildings. The Microchip team was brought in to help them design the electronics to control the speed of an electrical motor that was key to the water recirculation system in the cooling towers.

This was a complex solution of providing both hardware and software key elements. That part of the project was all consuming for the local field engineers team. However, in the discovery process they have learned the power of asking the simple question, "What else?"

This first question usually leads naturally to more questions like this:

*What else in the implementation of your solution are you finding challenging?*

*What else in the execution of getting this product completed ON TIME is becoming a concern?*

*What else are you struggling to apply resources to solving?*

These questions can be both specific and general. Note that these questions are all opening up the possibility of discovering more complexity, more complications and more challenges that need solutions. On occasion, the best question is nothing more than just that: "What else?" And let it stand. Silence is golden – do not say another word until the client leads off.

With this client the team found that What Else opened up several key facts that needed resolution. The system that the client needed to create also needed to be able to communicate to the outside world with respect to issues that were flagged by the system itself. The data on usage needed to be stored in a remote location for use in determining cost of system operation over time, and that data needed to be accessible from the end client's mobile applications. All of this was in a different part of the system-requirements from the motor control space where they started.

The What Else dialog between the sales team and the client opened up greater opportunities to meet solution needs. By engaging with them at the maximum level of complexity that they could uncover, they also became a Trusted Advisor resource to them. The client came back on many occasions, even when it was known that Microchip did not have an existing product to address their identified needs.

In this complex world, filled with complicated demands, tricky situations, knotty problems and unclear ways forward, we need navigators who can lead us through to the best solutions. When the path is clear and there are few options along the way, we don't need anybody to help us get there. The most valuable sales professionals aren't afraid of complexity. Instead, they are experts in navigating and leading their clients through it.

When you see the opportunity in complexity and work through it with simple navigation, your clients appreciate the expert guidance, and your organization benefits from your skill in differentiation on more than price alone.

The first step is in shifting out of our comfort zone with simpler situations and not being afraid to step out into navigating complex needs and developing complex solutions. When we are ready to roll up our sleeves and really dig into "what else" is going on, we set ourselves up perfectly for the next big shift we need to make: **creating and delivering personalized insight.**

# SHIFTABILITY NOW: EMBRACING COMPLEXITY

## KEY TAKEAWAYS

- Don't fear complexity; complex problems and solutions offer more opportunity than simple ones.
- Complex problems are probably overwhelming your clients and they will likely welcome expert navigation through complicated situations.
- Complex problems may require complex solutions.
- Complex problems demand clear, simple navigation and communication.
- Discover opportunities to explore greater complexity through asking What Else questions.

## SHIFTABILITY MINDSET

1. What are you avoiding in your own life because it seems too complex? (Retirement planning, challenging relationships, difficult decisions...)
2. Where have you missed opportunities or what have you left on the table because you are relying on keeping it too simple?
3. What limiting beliefs are you holding about complex situations or problems? (Remember limiting beliefs may be false or they may be true. Ask yourself, what else is true?)

## SHIFTABILITY ACTION

In the next client engagement plan that you create, build two different "What Else" questions that are specific to their world and the discussion taking place - and ASK THEM. Just two. Don't go into interrogation mode. Just ask caring, thoughtful, helpful, questions. Then be quiet and listen. Practice the art of Golden Silence, which is that time after a question is tabled and you say NOTHING. NOTHING. The client must speak first, no matter how long that takes, and that can seem to be forever.

Six

# Packaging Eureka

## SHIFTABILITY #3: CREATING PERSONALIZED INSIGHT

An effective and relevant sales professional co-creates personalized insight.

Eureka – I have found it!

*ARCHIMEDES*

Creativity and insight almost always involve
an experience of acute pattern recognition:
the eureka moment in which we perceive the
interconnection between disparate concepts or
ideas to reveal something new.

*JASON SILVA, FILMMAKER AND PUBLIC SPEAKER*

Tailoring is a dying art, specifically bespoke tailoring, the highest form of custom menswear. Rory Duffy, a fifth generation, Savile Row-trained Master Tailor, is one of the last of his kind. Becoming a Master Tailor requires at least seven years' training, first as an apprentice to a Master, learning the craft of fitting, pattern making, cutting, and sewing. A bespoke suit is made from a pattern created from scratch, hand-cut and hand-sewn; it is specially handmade by a tailor for a particular person.

In this day and age, most of us would have more experience with ready-to-wear or off-the-rack clothing. Off-the-rack (OTR) suits are mass-produced in a factory, machine-cut and machine sewn to standardized sizes for the general market. These OTR suits are sold through retailers that may offer "tailoring", which is in reality just alterations to make minor adjustments to fit.

In between the off-the-rack suit and the bespoke suit, there is the option of getting a made-to-measure (MTM) suit. A suit that is made-to-measure is sewn from standard sized base pattern that is adjusted to the personal measurements of the client. Your measurements are taken and sent to the factory where your suit is machine-cut and made. You will likely be able to choose your fabric from a curated selection and have a short list of options to customize your suit. A made-to-measure suit is a customized factory-produced product.

If you would ever have the chance to commission a true bespoke suit, you would immediately notice the difference in the final product and through the whole experience. You will have multiple fittings with the tailor, each fitting adjusting and building on what's learned and discovered as the suit is constructed to fit every portion and proportion of your frame. The final product will be of the highest quality with fine details like hand-sewn buttonholes. And, as you would expect, a bespoke suit commands a higher price, reflecting the high degree of skilled work required.

The production of off-the-rack clothing is highly scalable, cheaper to produce and very easy to replicate. You can go to any clothing store and find something that will generally suit your needs. Made-to-measure clothing is also scalable but delivers a more individualized product for a higher price.

Bespoke tailoring is highly customized, more time consuming to produce, and difficult to scale or replicate.

"Bespoke is a collaboration between the tailor and client. Together they develop and create a style, fit and collection that's solely for the individual," says Rory, our Master Tailor.

So, why this sartorial lesson?

Because to be a truly effective master sales professional today you need to become a Master Tailor of a different sort, creating bespoke solutions built on highly personalized insight.

## A LITTLE INSIGHT ON INSIGHT

**Insight** is an important word in sales today. In today's world of commoditized products with little differentiation, being able to deliver unique and valuable insight to your clients is what is going to set you apart from the competition.

In *The Challenger Sale*, Matt Dixon and Brent Adamson note that often clients don't actually know what they need. In fact, their greatest need is to find out exactly what they need. Instead of trying to interrogate to discover how our solutions might fit, we can tell our clients what they need and give them insights into how they can think differently about their business.

Insight is information – unique knowledge that you can bring to the client that teaches them something new that may reframe what they are already thinking or open up a new train of thought. This knowledge or insight combined with your unique products can create a highly differentiated solution that delivers a competitive advantage for your and for your client. In fact, although many say that solution selling has been replaced by insight selling, we think insight selling is all about being the very best of solution sellers. Effective insight selling delivers higher order solutions, carefully crafted around client-specific insight and impact. Done well, it is the highest evolution of solution selling.

Insight delivery is a central tenet to *The Challenger Sale*, which Brent and Matt describe as "Commercial Teaching." They identify four key rules of effective commercial teaching that leads to more business:

1. Lead to your unique strengths.
2. Challenge customer's assumptions.
3. Catalyze action.
4. Scale across customers.

In other words, make sure that your insight brings something new to the client, that it points to a solution you can actually provide, and that it leads them to making a decision. The idea of scaling across customers suggests creating insight in a central marketing hub that is then delivered to targeted clients by the marketing team.

This idea of scalable insight is taking hold across the new landscape of selling. In effect, some companies are creating Insight Factories that identify customer needs, script conversations, define solutions and deliver a choreographed plan for customer engagement that a sales rep simply has to execute. These factory-generated insights can be reasonably effective to a point. They are just not the MOST effective. Consider the story of Grainger in *The Challenger Sale*.

The Grainger story was about how they developed a specific insight and service that they could offer their client base by understanding the clients' purchasing patterns. This insight was carefully researched and created and as it was delivered to the first clients, it represented a whole new way of thinking. It positioned Grainger as a strategic partner instead of just a transactional supplier and it offered a great difference to the client – until their nearest competitor also offered the same insight and service. So that great new way of thinking just became commoditized, and again price became the only discussion point.

Because pretty much anything made in a factory can be commoditized.

Just like an off-the-rack suit, off-the-shelf insights can eventually be replicated by the competition and your differentiation is lost. You are back to where you started, with everyone packaging and selling the same solution, selling the same suit.

The real difference maker that we need to focus on is the **Tailor** part of *The Challenger* learning. You can take that insight that has been corporately created by the brain trust at the Insight Factory and use it as is. It will work for a while. Then it will wither as your competitors catch up and start to deliver the same insight and same solutions. Instead, if you can take that insight and *tailor* it to the specific client that you are serving and their specific needs, you will be delivering unique, valuable difference-making insight.

Through carefully understanding the impact that your insight will have on your client and their business, you can create a **client-specific version** of the factory insight and your advantage will last a bit longer. How long you keep your advantage depends on how well you tie in multiple aspects of your solution to multiple needs of the client. We could call this Made-to-Measure insight creation — still taking advantage of the efficiencies of scaling production while delivering a more individualized solution, like a made-to-measure Brooks Brothers suit. It fits better than a suit off the rack but it isn't too time-consuming to produce.

But ultimately, the best solutions and best outcomes are achieved through what is really bespoke tailored insight: **insight that is highly personalized to a specific individual within your client**.

Developing and packaging truly personalized insight requires a lot of hard work, great focus on the client and specific wisdom about how your solutions can uniquely serve them. This is a high bar to set for the average sales professional, which is why many feel that creating an Insight Factory is the only way to get it done. They simply believe it is too much to expect. Perhaps they are right.

Creating and selling insight and solutions does require greater skills than selling the simple features and benefits model of transactional sales. That is why we are writing this book — and why you are reading it. This is the new frontier of selling and sales reps that master these skills will be the ones who survive and thrive.

Now, ideally you will have some organizational support from your company in crafting your insight and teaching messages, but ultimately the heavy lifting comes down to you, the sales professional. And although it may seem daunting, mastering the art of insight delivery is simpler than trying to become an expert in all the features and benefits of all your solutions. The art of insight delivery depends simply on building great connection and having effective conversations. Personalized insight is co-created, developed and delivered through you working with a specific individual in the client company, just like a bespoke suit is a collaboration between tailor and client to create the perfect fit and style.

## CREATING PERSONALIZED INSIGHT

The insights and solutions that we bring to our clients need to be centered on one or more of the three main goals that every company is trying to reach:

1. Grow their revenue
2. Reduce their total costs
3. Manage their risks

Every interaction that we have with a client must be aimed at serving them in one of those three areas. We become valuable by helping the client see the same old things in a brand new light, through the insights we bring to them. We can start at the outer level of industry insights related to trends we are observing, events on the horizon or the economy at large. The next level of insight is specific to the client company and what's happening in their world, with their competitors, their unique challenges and economic drivers. Then we come to the level of the individual buyer or stakeholder we are working with and the opportunity to create, discover and tailor insights specific to them and their role and their context.

## HALLMARKS OF PERSONALIZED INSIGHT

### 1. IT IS DISCOVERED, NOT JUST DELIVERED.

We have used the term insight delivery, which sounds like we show up with a packaged bit of brilliance, deliver the designed a-ha moment and dazzle the client into action. This is exactly how many expect insight selling to work.

In reality, developing insight is a process of discovery. Real insight must be discovered through great two-way conversations that matter to both parties.

Conversation is as much about *listening* as it is about telling, perhaps even more so. Real insight is an unpredictable outcome of creative minds exposing and exploring the reality of the business involved. You cannot predetermine where you will go with the thinking. You only know that the first path you start down will likely lead to a different path where you will discover the most value.

We see this unfold in the field regularly through the thoughtful give and take of intentional conversation. Offer a small insight early in the conversation, build a little curiosity around it, then get a mini invitation to expand on the conversation and start the process again, and again. All while listening carefully for the insights the client has to offer to the process.

In one case Mitch was having a conversation with an engineering manager at a client. They had talked about helping the client shorten their time to market by bringing added resources to the project where they knew they could help in specific areas. This would shorten their development time by several weeks and launch the product sooner. Mitch and his team knew this, because they had seen the same problem before and they had the data to back up their assumptions.

Mitch asked the client if there was a future plan for a revision of the project as he suspected that a couple of key components from other manufacturers might be at risk for obsolescence. Mitch explained that through their own research with their client base of over 100,000, they had determined that more than 30% of their clients redirect more than 30% of their new product development resources to redesign teams to fix problems caused when other semiconductor companies stopped manufacturing components that they had made for years.

They had also learned that each one of those system redesigns typically cost the client $150,000. That is a lot of resources and money spent on projects just to tread water. Mitch was standing in front of a white board jotting these numbers down on the board and talking to each point. Mitch then handed the client the marker and ask how that might compare to his current situation. They had delivered some data that built credibility and encouraged curiosity to continue the conversation. This also enabled him to take that data to his management team to make sure that there were available resources to handle the contingencies.

## 2. IT IS CO-CREATED WITH THE CLIENT.

When Mitch handed the client the marker he invited him into the process as a collaborator, instead of being a mere recipient of information. While information like that is powerful on its own, we continually see that the co-creation of that learning experience is normally just the starting point of a much more open and conversational relationship that serves everyone better.

The process of insight discovery and development really needs to be collaborative with your client. Only through working with them will you discover the opportunities to address their specific needs and pain points. The skills of creating connection and nimbly applying different modes of client engagement are vital, as is your willingness to wade into complex situations. Effective collaboration depends on careful listening, asking good questions and a genuine curiosity to explore.

## 3. IT IS TAILORED TO A SPECIFIC PERSON WITHIN THE CLIENT COMPANY.

The best of all outcomes are achieved when you, as a serving professional, co-create insight that applies to a **specific person** within the client. It applies to that person as an individual and what they are working to achieve. It applies to that person as a stakeholder and where they are in the client decision-making process and the progression of that process. This personalization is the most powerful connection that you will make at a client.

This brings us back around to the idea of purpose. The ability to create a uniquely tailored solution built on personalized insight hinges on your understanding of purpose in all its facets including corporate, role and individual for yourself and for your client. And like a master tailor, you have to care deeply about the work you are doing and the difference you can make for someone else.

Think about the person you work with in a client-company. This person has specific needs and objectives that are unique to them. You have the opportunity to help them in ways that go beyond the overall business aims of their company. How can you help them do their job better? What constraints are pushing on them personally? What obstacles can you help remove? Can you help them meet deadlines? What information can you provide that impacts this person, not just this company?

Remember the story of the industrial controls engineer who was also coaching his son's little league team? We have another similar story, but this time the client was coaching soccer.

Mitch was calling on "Jim", an engineer at a medical device client that they had been serving for years. Jim was a young father of three with his oldest son just turning ten. In this case, Jim was involved in the software creation of a new medical device that was due to market in the next few months. He had used Microchip products and software tools to develop their end products on many occasions. This time out the pressure to get the product to market was particularly high.

Added to the work pressure was the fact that Jim had just volunteered to coach his son's soccer team. And that was a BIG community involvement in this case. Mitch listened carefully to the conflicting needs for him to push to work overtime and at the same time to coach his son's soccer team. Mitch's team had multiple solutions. They arranged for an outside consultant to assist in the project. They also coordinated their own technical experts locally and from the factory across the continent to help create the framework for the software and provided key sections of pre-written software code to address some of the special functions needed. They assisted further by helping with the quality assurance and compliance testing needed to get this medical device to market perfectly. On the personal side Mitch was able to reach out internationally and connect Jim with a youth coaching expert that one of the European team members knew well.

In this case, the team delivered highly personalized insight and solutions that helped the client meet his corporate mandate and see through his personal commitment to his son. That's how you work with your client to truly make a difference.

Insight is good. Personalized insight is invaluable.

# FROM INSIGHT TO ACTION

Earlier in this chapter we noted one of the most important rules about creating insight from *The Challenger Sale*: the insight you generate should **catalyze action.** As Matt and Brent note, "It's not enough to change the way customers think. You've ultimately got to get them to act."

The ability to move a client toward making a decision and into action is at the core of the next Shiftability skill: **leveraging and managing tension**.

# SHIFTABILITY NOW: CREATING PERSONALIZED INSIGHT

## KEY TAKEAWAYS

- While insight is good, personalized insight invaluable.
- Personalized insight is discovered, not just manufactured and delivered.
- Personalized insight will be co-created with the client.
- It is tailored to the specific person with whom you are working.
- Effectively creating personalized insight depends on understanding purpose, creating connection and willingness to engage with complex situations.
- Mastering the art of personalized insight requires a lot of hard work but will set you apart as a true sales professional

## SHIFTABILITY MINDSET

The fear of engaging with people at a very personal level can be quite daunting. To do this well you must really care about creating a different outcome than everyone else. That caring requires commitment to preparation, understanding of the real value that your company delivers, and a lot of work. Commit yourself to making a true difference with people and your client will see that.

1. What other limiting beliefs could hold you back from developing and creating personalized insight? (Remember limiting beliefs may be false or they may be true. Ask yourself, what else is true?)
2. Think of the clients with whom you are currently working. What constraints are they under? Make a list of your clients' challenges and brainstorm on some ways you can tailor solutions to their needs.

## SHIFTABILITY ACTION

Take your most critical client relationship and look for just ONE solution point that you can take from the fundamental old world way of thinking in terms of features and benefits, and make it personally valuable to just one person within the client. Understand how it will truly affect that person, good or bad. Understand what it will mean to them, personally AND professionally. Plan a very complete 2-way conversation with that client. And if you can't find that kind of valuable component to your offering, start over and rethink how you have positioned your service.

Seven

# Is It Warm in Here?

## SHIFTABILITY #4: LEVERAGING AND MANAGING TENSION

An effective and relevant sales professional uncovers, leverages and manages tension towards action.

> I must confess that I am not afraid of the word 'tension.' I have earnestly opposed violent tension, but there is a type of constructive, non-violent tension, which is necessary for growth.

> Martin Luther King Jr. — A letter from Birmingham Jail

> The world is all gates, all opportunities, strings of tension waiting to be struck.

> Ralph Waldo Emerson

Tension is not something we generally seek out. Tension in situations and in relationships is usually at best uncomfortable and at worst leads to open conflict. Instead, our instinct is to reduce tension, remove tension, and avoid tension whenever possible. We are well conditioned to seek conflict-free and harmonious interactions.

The irony is harmony depends entirely on tension. Have you ever tried to play a guitar that was out of tune? If the strings are too loose or too tight, the guitar isn't going to sound very good. The strings have to be carefully tuned to the right level of tension to produce the desired notes.

Tension is fundamental to existence. The laws of physics show us this. Too little tension and things fall apart, too much tension and things snap. Tension itself is a neutral thing, neither good nor bad. It is how tension is managed that determines the outcome.

Similarly, in sales, skillfully managing tension is key to producing the results you need. Every negotiation includes tension between collaborative relationship and competitive self-interest. Sales people often mistakenly believe that their job is to remove tension. Removing tension feels better than managing it. But when we remove the tension, we remove the dynamic energy that moves people to make decisions and commitments.

We just finished discussing the importance of creating and delivering personalized insight for the client. The risk of delivering insight is that the client can feel that value has been received and the momentum of the conversation stalls there. When we have a eureka moment, our brain rewards us for the insight as if we have already changed our behavior and it removes the urgency to take action. When you deliver insight without leveraging tension to move toward action, you end up giving away free consulting.

Tension is also the energy that drives creativity in negotiations, which is necessary for designing solutions that will satisfy the interests and needs of both parties.

Remember the Point A to Point B diagram from Chapter 2; in the discussion of transformation we talked about moving from our current reality and behavior (Point A) to our desired behavior and future (Point B). In the same way your client is at Point A, at the beginning of a tension bridge. Your job is to manage the conversation and move your client across that tension bridge to Point B, which is your desired outcome. To do that you will need to be comfortable with tension.

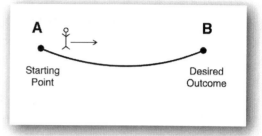

## GETTING COMFORTABLE WITH TENSION: FIGHT OR FLIGHT

There are four typical responses to tense situations: fight, flight, freeze or fawn.

Some people are drawn to conflict. They are itching for a fight and at the slightest provocation the gloves come off. Others will turn and run from it as fast they as can. The third response to is to freeze and shut down. Finally, the "fawn" response is perhaps the most insidious. This is the person who will do anything to fix the tension. They will give up and give in to everything just to make everyone feel better.

All of these responses are disastrous in sales negotiations. You simply can't pick a fight, run away, shut down or give it all up and be successful. For most sales people, the natural response to increased tension is to become either too collaborative or too competitive. Instead, you must shift into being comfortable with tension, and learn how to **engage** with it. Engaging tension includes planning for it, recognizing it and managing it.

Please note that we are not advocating that you look for ways to create conflict. Any jerk can do that. Tension and conflict are two different things. It is also important to note that tension is always there; you don't have to artificially create it. Your job is simply to reveal it and transform it into a decision to buy, not to remove it or avoid it. This transformation of tension into something constructive involves both raising and lowering the tension at different points as you move the client toward action. We are going to show you ways to increase and decrease people's experience of tension but first we need to talk about your role in the selling and negotiation process.

# MANAGING CONSTRUCTIVE TENSION AND CONFLICT

## STAY NEUTRAL

The first thing you must do is shift yourself into a neutral place and depersonalize the tension that is there. This means that while you still experience the tension, you do not own it. The minute you hook into the tension and it becomes yours, you become positional instead of neutral.

Position is not the same as interest. What does that mean? Let's illustrate. Two boys are fighting over the last orange in the market. Each of them is holding the same position: "I must have the orange." The shop owner asks the first boy why he needs the orange. "I need the juice for my sick sister," the boy answers. The shop owner asks the second boy why he needs the orange. "I need the peel for the cake my mother is baking," the second boy answers. Suddenly we see a potential solution emerging because each of them has a different *interest* in the orange.

When you stay neutral instead of positional you will be better able to manage the tension towards finding the creative solution that satisfies the interests that are represented. If you get hooked by the tension and start to own it yourself you will be tempted to alleviate it too soon. You don't want to remove the tension because without tension there won't be a decision; the goal is to manage the tension.

## REPOSITION AND OBJECTIFY THE CONVERSATION

From your neutral position you can now reposition and objectify the conversation. Remember: every negotiation includes tension between collaborative relationship and competitive self-interest. Tension is always there in varying levels – you are simply revealing and transforming it into a decision. The first step is to determine what level of tension is in the current engagement. We like this scale that we've adapted from Perry Holley, which ranks five levels of tension.

## 1. APATHY

At this level we are basically asleep and completely unaware of any problem.

**Key Phrase:** Do something? I don't need to do anything - everything is just fine.

**Key Word:** Zzzzzzzzzz

## 2. POWER PASSIVITY

Awareness is growing that there may be an issue but there is a reluctance to do anything.

**Key Phrase:** I know I need to do something. I just wish someone else would do it.

**Key Word:** Delegate or Avoid

## 3. POWER STATE

There is clearly a problem but we're not sure what we are going to do about it.

**Key Phrase:** I know I need to do something – but I haven't decided what yet.

**Key Word:** Shopping

## 4. POWER STRESS

We understand the problem and we are working on the solution.

**Key Phrase:** I know what I need to do and I am going to do it now!

**Key Word:** BUY!!

## 5. STRESSED

The problem is too much and we need you to fix this for us.

**Key Phrase:** Tell me what to do! I don't know what to do! Fix it now!

**Key Word:** Panic

Your client will be somewhere on this scale of tension. You want to remove the tension from between you and your client, to between them and the decision they need to make. This starts with creating connection as we discussed in the chapter on situational engagement. Figuratively, or literally, you move from opposing each other across the table to being shoulder-to-shoulder, considering together the problem in front of you. You may find it helpful to actually write things on a white board. Depersonalizing and objectifying the conversation this way allows to you to build the tension between them and the possible solution while you remain neutral. You still feel the tension, but it's not yours because you don't have to make the decision.

Depending where your client is on the scale you may need to manage the tension up or down. If they are down in the depths of apathy with no incentive to buy, you are going to need to ratchet up the tension to move them to action. If they are in full panic mode screaming for a price reduction, you need to bring the tension down to move them into a more rational decision-making mode.

## WAYS TO LOWER TENSION

1. **Normalize**
   Acknowledge their circumstances and affirm the person. Don't tell them to relax. Show compassion. Use phrases like *I understand* or *I can see that this is tough.*

2. **Simplify**
   Create order and provide structure. Give people a sense of security. If your client is in full panic mode, say calmly, "We're going to do three things…" and lay out a plan.

3. **Add or Restore Resources**
   Offer to bring in an expert or to have your R&D team look at the problem. But don't change the merit of the deal by throwing in additional product. You are trying to ease the feeling of tension, not change the deal.

## WAYS TO RAISE TENSION

1. **Bring a little bad news.**
   Increase the insecurity of the status quo.

2. **Say the hard thing no one else is willing to say.**
   Tell the truth; call it like it is. It is more important to be respected than to be liked.

3. **Highlight the contrast between now and what could be.**
   *Your competition is more differentiated and you're late to market. But what if you could be first to market?*

4. **Remove resources.**
   *We've spent 3 months on this project with you and management is telling me I have to move my team on to the next project.*

5. **Leave the table.**
   Be prepared to walk away. This is a legitimate possibility that will usually force a decision one way or another.

So what does this all look like in action? Let's take a look at a hostage situation, where the entry point is establishing the exit point.

## A HELICOPTER AND A MILLION DOLLARS

The principles of negotiating in a hostile situation, like a hostage taking, provide an excellent framework for understanding how to manage tension in a sales context. (You may be nodding very sympathetically here.) Let's watch how this unfolds.

A hostage negotiator generally enters the situation unarmed, showing that he is not there to overpower. He is neutral and he is there to find a solution and reset or redirect the situation. The very first thing he does upon entering the situation is **find the exit**.

*When you start a sales negotiation, you start from a neutral position and you have to know your own exit. What is your walk-away? At what point will you exit the deal?*

The next step is for the negotiator to **establish a connection and open communication** with the hostage-taker. Of course, the hostage-taker demands a million dollars and a helicopter. (Hostage-takers always demand a million dollars and a helicopter; clients always demand a price reduction.) The negotiator then works to stabilize the situation and **lower** the tension.

He acknowledges the demand: "Thank you for talking to me. Okay, you want a helicopter and a million dollars."

He affirms the person: "I can see that you are in a tough situation here, Jim. This is not easy for you."

Then he redirects the conversation and creates order: "First, we are going to do three things…"

Then he might add some resources: "Let's get you some water and pizza."

*As you open communication with your client, you probably already know their position: "You have to give us a price decrease!"*

*You acknowledge the request, affirm them and then pivot and redirect the conversation. "Okay, I can see that price is important here and we will talk about that in a bit. But first, let's discuss what we can do about getting to market earlier."*

Our negotiator has successfully lowered the tension and stabilized the situation. Now, he moves to discovering Jim's interests versus his position. "What brought you here today, Jim? What's your story?"

*This is where you probe to understand what is behind your client's position. "Why do you need a price reduction? What are the pressures you are under? What do you need to get out of this?"*

Now, the negotiator needs Jim to release the hostages and surrender, so he starts ratcheting the tension back up. "Jim, there are snipers with guns aimed at your head right now. You have the choice to come out of this dead, or alive. It's up to you."

*Once you have identified the actual interests behind your client's position, you can start raising the tension towards action or decision. "We can get you to market earlier, if we can get started on this deal right now."*

The outcome in both our hostage situation and our sales negotiation is entirely contingent on how well the negotiator manages the tension, not on completely removing it. Removing the tension leaves both situations in an intolerable stalemate. Poorly managed tension can result in catastrophe – dead hostages and dead deals. Successfully managing the tension can lead to the hostages being released – and to finding creative solutions in sales negotiations.

## TENSION OR CONFLICT?

We will close this chapter with a final note on the idea of destructive tension versus constructive tension. Constructive tension is the energy that powers action and decision, and fuels creative solutions that address multiple interests. Destructive tension demoralizes, picks fights and fosters conflict with the aim not so much on winning, but rather on destroying the opponent.

We have noted the rising prevalence of hostile negotiating tactics in today's business environment. When someone is trying to outmaneuver you using harsh manipulation techniques it is more important than ever to maintain your neutral position.

In judo, the first lesson is on how to use the other person's energy to shift them off balance. In a hostile negotiating situation, use all the energy available to shift the scenario. One of the first hostage negotiation rules is, "Never resist people's resistance." Stay neutral and redirect. When someone is trying to provoke conflict it reveals that they have a position. Look to uncover, understand and leverage that tension.

Getting comfortable with managing tension is not the easiest thing to do, simply because it is uncomfortable. This shift is especially hard for those who are skilled relationship builders. The problem is these relationship builders are often, in reality, just trusted advisors loved by their clients, who never sell anything.

If you overcome your discomfort and master the shift of skillfully uncovering, leveraging and managing tension toward the sale you can be a trusted advisor and insight provider who makes things happen.

And you will have the foundation in place for one of the most important yet elusive skills in sales: asking for the business.

# SHIFTABILITY NOW: MANAGING TENSION

## KEY TAKEAWAYS

- Tension is the necessary energy that moves people towards making decisions.
- It is not our job to remove tension but to manage it, both raising it and lowering it as needed.
- Tension is the source of the creativity needed to find solutions that will satisfy multiple interests.
- It is easy to become too collaborative or too competitive. To effectively manage tension it is necessary to stay neutral.

## SHIFTABILITY MINDSET

1. What is my natural reaction to tension? Fight, flight, freeze or fawn? How has that worked for me?
2. What limiting beliefs do I have about tension in sales negotiations? (Remember limiting beliefs may be false or they may be true. Ask yourself, what else is true?)
3. When have I become positional in a sales negotiation? What happened?

## SHIFTABILITY ACTION

1. Prior to your next client engagement, identify a couple of ways you will stay neutral. What will you say? What will you not say?
2. Is there a client where you need to raise the tension a bit to move them towards a decision? Identify 3 ways you could do that with your team.

Eight

# Can I Take Your Order, Please?

## SHIFTABILITY #5: ASKING FOR THE BUSINESS

**An effective and relevant sales professional understands the power and importance of request.**

You miss 100% of the shots you don't take.

*WAYNE GRETZKY*

If you don't go after what you want, you'll never have it. If you don't ask, the answer is always no. If you don't step forward, you're always in the same place.

*NORA ROBERTS*

For many years, a key part of training at Mitch's annual sales meetings has been the sales pitch competition. An entire week would be spent together learning about new products, new solutions, and the latest technologies and how to communicate the features and benefits effectively. Then everyone would be grouped into teams of 6-8 people and take on the challenge of preparing the new product pitch and building the next great customer presentation.

The sales teams would then meet with mock "client teams" and compete to see who could deliver the best pitch. Over several days 30-40 teams would make their pitch to the panel of judges.

The prime criterion for judging this sales competition amongst very seasoned global sales professionals was simply this:

**Did they ask for the order?**

And you know what... *less than half of them would ever actually ask for the order.*

While you would think that was the most elementary thing for a sales professional to do, it turns out that asking for the order is something many people avoid or simply do not do well. In this chapter, we are going to explore why we don't ask for the business and then discuss new ways of thinking that will help develop this very important skill.

Up to this point we have been discussing the shiftability skillset for managing the sales process today:

We have learned how to be nimble and **match appropriate styles of sales engagement to the situation and people at hand.**

We have recognized that **complexity creates opportunity** and helps us take the conversation beyond price to exploring true value.

We have seen that the creation and delivery of **personalized insight** is the best way to deliver true value.

And we understand that **tension is essential** for moving from insight to action.

Too often sales people get stuck right here, managing a perpetual sales process, busy creating value, and they never quite get to the point of asking for the business. This can be especially true in complex sales, which require a long engagement, often up to 18 months.

We have seen this over and over again in the field and in training. In thousands of simulations just like the annual sales meeting competitions, and in real client engagements, too many sales people **simply do not ask for the business**.

## WHY WE DON'T ASK

What is it that keeps us from asking for something? Most often we are afraid of the answer because it might be one we don't like. Once we ask for something we give the power of decision making to the client. There is now the possibility they will say no. Or they might say yes – which can also be stressful. Asking for the business is essentially drawing a line in the sand and asking to move into the next dimension, which can be uncomfortable whether the answer is yes, no, or not yet.

We also may be afraid of losing control; if we stay in the process phase we can hold on to the illusion that we are in the driver's seat. So we might make a feeble attempt at asking by saying something like, "We should probably go to the next step." A statement like this is not actually asking for anything; it's simply broadcasting a need. It's like saying, "I'm hungry" and hoping your spouse will make you dinner, instead of asking, "Could you make me some dinner?"

So we avoid the stress of moving into the next phase by prolonging the sale and staying busy in the comfortable development phase. But our job in sales is to manage tension towards action and decision, as we just saw in the previous chapter – not to be keeping everyone comfortable.

When we draw the line in the sand and make a clear request for action on the client's part there are three possible answers. Leading up to this point you have been working to create value, create connection and open up possibility. And, if you have done your job well, the client should have clarity, insight and some level of urgency to get something done.

The first possible answer is No, or they may retreat back into negotiation on price. Obviously we fear this answer because no one likes to fail. Fear of failure is a huge reason we stay in the development process and avoid the threshold of decision.

The next possible answer is Not Yet. This answer brings a lot of uncertainty and can mean yes or no. It requires clarification and means that we need to do some more work, perhaps a lot more work, and we may need to start over and redo all the work we have already accomplished. And all of this work may just bring us to another No.

The last possible answer is Yes. We would expect that this is the answer we all want to hear, but some people fear success like they fear failure because this adds work of a different kind. The move into the execution phase can be daunting. Many people who avoid asking for a decision probably don't have a well-developed post-close process with clear steps for paperwork, transitioning to account management and verifying that they have delivered value. It is also not uncommon that someone in sales might feel a sense of loss or purpose once the deal is won. A lot of people thrive on the energy of the process, much like someone who enjoys the hunt but doesn't like the kill.

There are other limiting beliefs and assumptions we make that hold us back from asking, regardless of the kind of answer we may expect. We may doubt our abilities. We may make assumptions about the buying power of the client. We may believe there are circumstances that will conspire against our success.

Success in asking especially requires examining the limiting beliefs we are holding about ourselves, about the client, about the deal, and about the circumstances surrounding it. And then going through the process of letting go of those limiting beliefs and finding new beliefs that will move us forward, as described in Chapter Two.

Finally, we may simply not know how to ask for something effectively. If you can master this shift into skilled asking, you will be in a rare group of sales leaders indeed. This requires some mind shifts about the nature of "closing" business.

## ASKING FOR A DECISION IS DIFFERENT THAN CLOSING

As sales people we hear it all the time – everything is about driving to The Close. *When are you going to close that deal? What do you need to do wrap this up?*

The majority of sales training for the last several decades has been focused on helping the sales person Close the Deal. There are techniques to Trial Close, to Pre-Close, to Soft Close, and even to Reverse Close. The Reverse Close is where you actually tell the client that you can certainly see that they are not yet ready to take advantage of this great offer, so let's just forget it for now – a bit of negative psychology that sadly works.

We need you to understand something very important: asking for something and closing are not the same thing.

In the world of complex selling and client relationships, asking for the order is not the endpoint – it is the **launch point** of the next phase or client engagement.

Right on the heels of getting the order, comes the verification process where our aim is to clearly get a shared understanding of the value that has been created in the client's eyes by the work that you have done. From the verification process you escalate the discussion to other needs that that were identified through the journey in the first transaction. And the cycle of client engagement starts again.

Shifting our thinking about The Close is critical. In the past The Close was seen as the grand finale. While once The Close was the end, now it's just another point on the way to this question: **What's next?**

## THE ART OF EFFECTIVE ASKING

There are many excellent resources that will teach you specific strategies for how to ask for the business. We want to highlight some basics and then show you some scenarios that will help you see how to overcome the things that hold you back from asking.

Effective asking depends on adequate preparation, knowing what to ask for, and knowing whom to ask.

## PREPARING FOR THE ASK

A skilled salesperson knows that everything in the sales engagement process is ultimately preparing for and driving to asking for the business. Having this end in mind helps direct and inform everything in your client engagement process to move towards making a commitment.

Preparation leading up to asking for a decision includes defining and agreeing on value together with the customer and verifying that it has been created. It means that you have done your homework and established and clarified the true need and how you will meet it. It is important to be specific and remove any ambiguity about next steps and clearly outline the why, how and what. It is very helpful to map out the next steps in a carefully defined post-ask process.

When you have gone through a process of engaging with your client to navigate through complex needs and solutions; to discover and co-create personalized insight and value; managed the tension to move them from panic or inaction to commitment and decision; and diligently prepared to define and verify the commitment you are asking them for, you are not in the position of begging for the sale. You have earned the right to ask for the business.

## KNOWING WHAT TO ASK

Part of the preparation for asking is knowing specifically what you are asking for. The substance of what you are asking for is moving from exploring possibility to making a commitment. But you need to plan the specific requests you are going to make. And be direct and clear about it. Avoid half-hearted implied requests like the spouse who says, "I'm hungry." Ask specifically for whatever form commitment takes in the space in which you are working.

*Can we sign a contract?*
*Can we issue the purchase order?*
*Can we draft an agreement?*

Even if you have done your job very well and worked brilliantly with your client you still have to ask for the PO, the contract, the agreement. It's not that complicated. Just plain and simple – **ask for the business**.

## KNOWING WHOM TO ASK

An important part of managing the client engagement process is making sure you are talking to the right people along the way.

Have you identified the decision makers and the ones who can mobilize the decision makers? It's easy to cultivate and build relationships with people who can't help you. Match the decision you are asking for to the right decision maker.

It's also easy to direct your request to someone who has no power to give you the business – because then it's not your fault when they can't give it to you.

Use the situational client engagement skills to make sure you are talking to the right people.

# AFTER THE REQUEST

As we described earlier there are basically three possible responses to a request for the business: Yes, Not Yet and No.

## WHEN THE ANSWER IS YES

This is, of course, the best possible outcome. Yahoo! You won the business! But don't celebrate too soon. In the semiconductor industry, only a quarter of design wins turn into revenue. Don't let the thrill of winning make you take your eyes off the ball. Be diligent in completing the post-ask process and then, of course, ask **what's next?** Move the momentum into the next level of client engagement and new business.

## WHEN THE ANSWER IS NOT YET

A Not Yet answer is a red flag that mainly suggests one of two things: 1) you haven't done your job well enough or 2) the client is not committed to the process. Assess where you may able to deliver more information or address some deficits: What else do you need? What's missing?

Then test their commitment to the deal and ask questions about why the variables have changed. Ask if they will commit to signing if you give them more time or provide what is missing. You can also try some creative solutions like suggesting that you sign a contract now that won't be enforced for 30 days.

There are cases where you have done a very good job but they simply may need more time or they need to change the variables. But it's always important to verify that this need is legitimate. They may still be "shopping", they may be using you to negotiate down with a competitor, or they may be reluctant themselves to say no even though that is the actual outcome. Saying no can be as difficult as hearing No.

## WHEN THE ANSWER IS NO

As we noted at the beginning, one of the biggest things that holds us back from asking is the fear of hearing No, so we simply don't ask to avoid that possibility. But to ask for the business successfully you have to acknowledge that No is a possible answer – and then know what to do with that.

Tension will inevitably follow asking for something and this tension can be uncomfortable, which is why we often try to avoid it. The tense period that follows asking is one of the times that it is especially vital to remain neutral. Remember, you can experience tension without owning it.

When you hear No, it's important to remember that it is just a word, and probably one to which we give too much power. No requires context to give it any substance. It can be a perceived wall maker, a conversation branch creator, or an absolute command. In the business of selling and or negotiating you have to get over the fear of hearing or saying No.

No can mean a variety of things. It can mean not now, or I'm not convinced yet or I have more questions. Today, with decisions often depending on consensus among multiple stakeholders, No can simply mean you haven't answered *everyone's* questions.

So No can simply be another data point that brings clarity and allows for some review and reflection.

Remember that No is usually not personal, even though it can feel like it is. People say No based on their context and their variables. Don't let the conversation about No become a conversation about yourself. Jim Camp, author of *Start With No,* offered this advice: "Stop trying to control the outcome, focus on your behavior and actions instead. Control what you can control, and forget the rest."

Nelson Mandela said, "I never lose. I win or I learn." This is the time to stop and review your engagement leading up to receiving the No. Did you engage with the client in the right way based on their role and their needs? Could you have asked better questions? Could you have prepared better and managed more effective conversations? Did you help the client navigate the complexity of their situation with simple and clear communication? Did you manage the tension appropriately?

But through all of this evaluation remember that this is about the value of the deal and the engagement, not the value of you. Stay neutral. Just like we're not human doings, we're not human deals. Ultimately the question is **what was missing in the deal**? Not – what was missing in me?

When one path ends in a No, then open another path with a revised plan and improved questions, each time gathering more understanding and information along the way.

## RESILIENCE

Learning to how deal with No is really about resilience. Can you get back up when you have been knocked down? Several years ago Hendre was brought in to a trading company to work with the traders on resilience.

Traders operate in a high stakes, high stress environment. A trading firm's success lies in the ability of the trader to make the right trade at the right time. The success of a trade is measured in the margin of profit they generate. Traders do their best to understand their markets, to be as informed as possible, and to make solid, predictable trades. The traders take risks with other people's money, but they are also personally at stake. The measured success of a trader is directly tied to their ability to take bigger risks. The bigger trade, the bigger the potential profit.

For a trader, the greater the risk, the greater the reward. But the inverse is true as well: the greater the risk, the greater the fall. The challenge was that many of the very successful traders would crash hard when they made a bad trade and disappear for days. Hendre's task was to work with the traders to increase their risk tolerance by increasing their resilience, or "bounce-back-ability", after a failure.

The main key to cultivating resilience was for the traders not to personalize the trade. Some of the traders began to believe that the reason they were successful was because they had secret knowledge and implicitly believed that they could influence the market. This led to superstitious thinking and things like wearing lucky pants or socks and attributing success or failure to following prescribed routines. This kind of magical thinking emerges in plenty of other occupations too.

The reality is trades are influenced by so many factors far beyond any one person's control. In trading you have to know that you **will** make bad trades. You simply cannot control everything. You can only take ownership for what you do and your commitment to a process. You can't take ownership of the decisions of those around you or factors beyond your control.

Similarly, in sales, you will not land every deal. People **will** say no. You have to stay neutral and not personalize the result. When we personalize the deal, we are no longer shiftable. If you detach yourself from the results, you will be able to learn how you can shift and adapt for the next one.

For the traders, their resilience depended on detaching themselves from the outcome of the bad trade and resetting themselves to their own commitment to their purpose: to get back out trading.

When the answer is No in sales, your resilience also depends on staying neutral and detaching yourself from the result; then reaffirming your own commitment and resetting to your own true north. A good question to ask is what am I committed to **creating**, instead of what am I committed to **getting**? Are you committed to selling a million dollar deal? Or are you committed to creating value and the possibility of generating a million dollars? Then you can attach yourself to things that are in your control. Then you can be flexible, shiftable and ready to bounce back to the next thing.

## ASKING FOR THE BUSINESS AND MY PURPOSE

If my purpose is to provide value to my client, I can't do that if I don't ask them to move to the next level and make a decision. If my purpose is to provide value to my company, I'm not doing that if I am giving away free consulting and not securing the deal. Ultimately, asking for the business is how your three-fold purpose fully connects to everything that you do in engaging with a client.

Don't get so busy applying new methods in the sales process that you stay there forever and forget the fundamentals – you have to ask for the business.

Don't underestimate the simple power of request.

Learn to be okay with the tension that inevitably follows making a request.

Learn how to respond and bounce back when No is the answer.

And remember that you can do everything "right" and still not get the business. Sometimes the signs are there in the beginning, if we know what to look for. And sometimes winning the business might not be worth it. That's what the next and last shift is all about.

# SHIFTABILITY NOW: ASKING FOR THE BUSINESS

## KEY TAKEAWAYS

- Asking for the business is a fundamental skill that needs practice.
- We can choose to stay in the process of sales engagement instead of moving towards action and commitment because we are afraid of failure. We can also be afraid of success.
- We need to shift our thinking about closing. Instead of seeing a decision as the endpoint, we need to understand that is a launch point to the next level of engagement, to the next opportunity with this client. Always be looking to **what's next.**
- You need to be prepared for the possible answers to your request for the business. Know how you will proceed when the answer is yes, know to respond and test when the answer is not yet, and know how to evaluate and bounce back when the answer is no.

## SHIFTABILITY MINDSET

1. Are you personalizing a no?
2. Where are you holding someone back from making a decision because you are afraid to ask?
3. What limiting beliefs are holding you back from asking for what you need?

## SHIFTABILITY ACTION

1. Take a look at your funnel or list of opportunities or pipeline – whatever you call it. Which engagements are past due for you asking for a decision?
2. Write down assumptions that you have made about that client or the deal. What has kept you from asking for the business?
3. Ask for the business anyway. Let them make their own decision.

Nine

# The Power of No

## SHIFTABILITY #6: KNOWING WHEN TO SAY NO AND HAVING THE COURAGE TO SAY IT

An effective and relevant sales professional has the courage to say no to things that don't make sense.

A 'No' uttered from the deepest conviction is better than a 'Yes' merely uttered to please, or worse, to avoid trouble.

MAHATMA GANDHI

I hate a man who always says 'yes' to me. When I say 'no' I like a man who also says 'no.'

SAMUEL GOLDWYN

Just say No.

NANCY REAGAN

**// The client has gone dark. Should I fly out?"** This was the anxious question a consultant recently posed to Hendre . This consultant had a potential client out of state and had been engaging through phone and email for about a year. Six months earlier the client had agreed on a Statement of Work. The consultant sent over the proposal and the client promised to sign it after the holidays.

Things dragged and the client delayed the decision. When the consultant asked to revisit the proposal the client came back saying, "We have had changes in the business. We will need a new proposal." So the client started the whole process again and put together a new proposal. Then the client went silent and dropped off the map.

"So should I fly out?" the consultant asked.

"What is the size of the deal?" Hendre asked.

"Fifty thousand dollars."

"Is this a final deal or is this an opening deal to a larger contract?" Hendre asked.

"It's the final deal," answered the consultant.

"Then I don't think it is worth a trip," Hendre said.

"But should I fly out?" pressed the consultant.

This was a classic case of the sunk cost fallacy. Sunk costs are payments or expenses that you can't get back or redeem. Economists argue that sunk costs should not affect a rational decision maker's choice, unlike fixed costs or prospective costs. We should make rational decisions based on the future value of objects, investments and experiences. But in reality, our decisions are often tainted by our past investments. The more we have put it into something, the harder it is to walk away, even when abandoning something is the most rational thing to do. This is what happens when we persevere through a miserable movie, "because I can't get my money back." Or we eat far past being comfortable in a restaurant, "because I paid for it." It's not rational to keep watching a horrible movie or to eat until we are sick, but the sunk cost fallacy negatively influences our behavior. Continuing to watch or eat does not redeem our sunk cost – it just makes us miserable. But somehow, we feel that is wrong to walk away.

In the case of the consultant, this client had been in his funnel for over a year. He had *invested* a lot of time, energy and expense in this client. He had sunk costs - he couldn't just walk away, even though the writing was on the wall that a deal was unlikely.

Hendre suggested that the consultant ask the client a litmus test question: "If I fly out will you sign the contract?"

If the answer is yes, then get on the plane.

If the answer is not yet or not sure, then this client *simply hasn't figured out how to say no.*

In the last chapter, we looked at how to respond when a client says no to us. But there are also times when we have to say no to our clients. And there are times when we have to help our clients say no and kick them out of the funnel. We have to say no to bad business and we have to recognize when the deal isn't going to happen and be willing to walk away from sunk costs, preferably sooner rather than later.

## HELPING CLIENTS MAKE DECISIONS

Our role is to help our clients make better decisions faster. A decision, whether it is yes or no, is preferable to indecision. Indecision leads to more work that can lead to more indecision. Remember that our role is to manage the tension to move clients from insight to action. Our ultimate end is to facilitate the buy. Our job is not done when the client is satisfied with the insight, but when we have delivered the product.

If a positive decision is not forthcoming but we haven't received a definitive no either, we may need to recognize that the client needs help saying no because he doesn't know how to do it.

Here are some signs that a client needs to say no.

- They keep changing the deal.
- They go dark.
- You're caught in perpetual negotiation.

- Another vendor is brought in.
- They are waffling in indecision.

At this point, if we have done our homework, we will have addressed any obstacles to a decision like needing more data, or a better price, or directing the decision to the actual decision maker. Once we have reiterated all of these things, if the client is still indecisive, we can create urgency by walking away with a statement like this: "I'm going to move on now. If you want to do this give me a call. I can keep this deal on the table for thirty days."

And sometimes, we might simply need to give them an out and ask if they need to say no.

The key is recognizing it's time to stop investment and having the courage to do it because continuing to invest in deals with poor potential is bad business.

## SAYING NO TO BAD BUSINESS

Common wisdom in sales is that everything we do has to be working towards getting to "yes." Everything you do is aimed towards getting the deal, getting the order, getting the signature, getting the yes.

And in fact, in the previous chapters we have been highlighting skills that we believe will lead to success in sales. Most people would judge success in sales simply by how many clients say "yes."

The problem is that if we are working to get yes from our clients at any cost, we can end up saying yes ourselves to the wrong things at a very high cost. When we are over-eager to please and close the deal it clouds our judgment and puts us in a very vulnerable position in negotiations. PICOS negotiators prey "on our old-fashioned, all American, Dale Carnegie instinct to win friends and influence people," says Jim Camp in his book, *Start with No.* Pretty soon, we discover that we have said yes to bad business.

The best sales professionals have the courage to say **no** to things that don't make sense, like annual price down negotiations, or unsustainable terms, or unreasonable demands. Simply, they can recognize bad business and walk away.

# WHY WE DON'T SAY NO

There are many things that hold us back from saying no when we need to. No is a hard thing to say to anyone. We might be afraid of losing our commission. We don't want to look like failures to our colleagues. We believe the bullying rhetoric of the hardline negotiators who try to shame us into submission. We don't want to risk damaging relationships that we have built. We are afraid of making the wrong decision. We can be intimidated by the potential consequences of no. And sometimes, we simply don't recognize bad business for what it is.

It is easier to find the courage to say no when you understand certain things.

## LEARN TO RECOGNIZE BAD BUSINESS.

Winning isn't always worth it – you simply cannot make up for bad business. If you capitulate and hand over price reductions that you can't sustain, sure, you might keep the client, but at what cost to your company? Will there still be a company when the next round of negotiations comes around?

Sometimes the signs are there right in the beginning that a deal is going to be a non-starter. Part of saying no effectively is getting out fast, before you have invested too heavily on a deal that is going nowhere or is going to cost too much.

We also have to be willing to make sure that there is real value in a deal for our company, not just our own numbers.

## RECOGNIZE MANIPULATION FOR WHAT IT IS

Most of the aggressive purchasing tactics fly under the banner of "working together for the win-win", which sounds like a good idea, until you realize you totally lost while helping them win.

The sad truth is threats and intimidation work most of the time so PICOS negotiators don't know what to do when you say you won't play their game. There have been many times when we have refused to participate in annual price down negotiations or to give in to other unreasonable demands. There is often a lot of threat and bluster but in the end we often still have the business. This leads to the next point.

## SAYING NO ISN'T NECESSARILY THE END

Walking away from a deal or refusing certain terms does not necessarily mean you are walking away from the client.

Mitch had been calling on a big electronics manufacturer for many years. They had always been a challenge to his team's pragmatic way of conducting business. To put it mildly, they were very demanding. This was not new and the industry all knew it. Over time this manufacturer had significantly raised the level of their demands in the area of the industry's social responsibility. This was a leading edge position and it was understandable that they chose to take this path. However, it was all but impossible for the industry to comply with the requirements they put forth.

Moreover, even if it could be followed, and that was a big if, the cost of doing so would have priced the products completely out of the market. At the same time, the client was telling Mitch that if they did not agree to the complete 200-page document on social responsibility, that they would not be doing business with this manufacturer in the future.

So they had to make a tough decision. They refused to comply with the unreasonable demands. However, this did not lead to losing the account as expected. They still do business with that client today.

Saying no is a risk, to be sure, but it often doesn't have the consequences that we fear.

## WALKING AWAY IS OKAY

The amazing power of walking away comes from the reality that a surprising amount of the time "walking away" will actually bring you back to the table. When you return it is most likely because the other party has called you back to the table. The power of no is huge. And it starts with the acceptance that it is okay for either party to take that position. If you want something more than the other side, then you are in a needy position and you will start compromising from the beginning. So here's a thought: don't negotiate. Put your best effort and offer on the table from the beginning and let it stand. If you put a compromise position on the table from the start, then you have just opened up the door for giving more.

One of the biggest challenges for the sales person is to stop investment. It's hard to walk away from that sunk cost. Many will continue forever in trying to knock down every brick wall encountered at a client. That diligence is admirable...and deadly. There is not enough time in the universe to do all that we need to do, so a correctly made disengagement with clients is appropriate. It needs to be done in concert with your leadership team and openly understood by all, even the client.

Walking away from stalled business and saying no to bad business is vital to your ultimate success as a sales professional. It's also vital to the success of your organization.

Mitch's sales team had been calling on a client for twenty years. They were doing tens of millions of dollars of business with them each year. Each year the client held their annual contract negotiations. And each year they set 5-10% price reduction expectations as targets. As the semi-conductor industry has matured, the practice of annual price reductions is no longer practical.

A decade ago, in the heydays of 20% growth per year, the industry had created the price reduction monster that they were now finding impossible to feed. Unprecedented growth had enabled lots of practices that were now unsustainable. For the previous two years the team had told this specific client that they would not be offering any price reductions at the annual contract "negotiation." That had caused quite a stir but in reality, there was no negative business or opportunity impact even though the client threatened that there would be a price to pay for not cooperating.

Many times Mitch carefully and respectfully explained the shift in the industry and how the best companies would have to make a shift from past practices. They had also spent many hours working with divisions other than purchasing and explaining the value contribution that they had in fact delivered all along the way.

It came to year three with the new "annual pricing" position. It was annual negotiation time again, and again they told the client that their price reductions would be zero. In fact, if Mitch's team was not going to be allowed to tell their value story as it applied specifically to what they had been able to jointly create with the client, they would simply not participate in the negotiations. They would be a no show. And according to the client, Mitch's team would be the ONLY no show.

They stood their ground and submitted a spreadsheet with zero price reductions for the "negotiation." A few weeks later they found themselves across the desk from the VP of Global Supply Chain Management for this client, having a terse discussion about their unacceptable stance. Again they explained the industry shift that had taken place, the new style of doing business that long term viable suppliers need to make, and how that meant there is no room for the outdated practice of annual price downs.

However, they explained, working together they could easily find system solutions that would exceed the savings that price downs would deliver. It would take working closely together, and it would deliver huge returns, many times greater than simply lowering price.

In response, the client leveled all the typical PICOS style threats. They were led to believe that they were the only suppliers "not playing ball" and that they were truly, deeply disappointed in the lack of professionalism and willingness to play win-win. Mitch's lack of competitiveness and cooperation would have to be elevated to their top management and they were certain that communication with his CEO would have to take place to let him know that Mitch's team was not meeting their reasonable needs. It got personal.

Mitch and his team had been down this path many times and the words were quite old and tired and represented nothing new and different. Threat, intimidation, manipulation, and personalization were all tactics they had learned to expect. While the team worked to talk about innovation and value they had delivered, each attempt just fell on closed ears.

The discussion came to a close with a final threat to have a CEO-to-CEO discussion about the team's unwillingness to cooperate.

"You know, the last time that happened our CEO actually raised all of the prices in discussion effective immediately which cost you 7% more," Mitch answered. "We can certainly arrange that discussion if you wish."

They simply said no. They took their ball and went home.

While the hope was that this conversation would end in a creative discussion about innovation and helping them solve problems that no one else could, this response put the close on the annual negotiation price down game. However, it didn't end the relationship and to this day they still work hard to provide value to this client.

## REMEMBER YOUR PURPOSE

Finding the courage to say no ultimately comes from understanding our own purpose. We have to be willing to do the right thing and serve value to both parties, first to our corporation and then to our client. In the end, saying yes to things that don't make sense won't deliver value to anyone.

If we go back to the premise that our role is to help clients make better decisions faster, whether it is yes or no, that can change our perspective on the sales funnel. It is a funnel of the client's decision-making process rather than a funnel of sales activity.

We don't win everything we work on. Not everything we win goes to revenue. Stuff falls out of the funnel on the way. Some things need to be kicked out of the funnel either because it's going nowhere, or because it's bad business. Finding the courage to say no and walk away when it is the right thing to do will ultimately set you up for greater success.

# SHIFTABILITY NOW: THE POWER OF NO

## KEY TAKEAWAYS

- To be successful in sales, you must be willing to say no to bad business.
- Don't let sunk costs hold you back from walking away from a deal that is not going anywhere.
- A client's indecision or stalled engagement may be signaling that they need to say no, but don't know how. Sometimes we need to help the client to say no.
- Recognize and resist manipulation and aggressive PICOS tactics.
- Saying no is not always the end. It can be powerful for creating urgency or jumpstarting stalled engagement.
- Walking away from something creates the space and opportunity for new business somewhere else.

## SHIFTABILITY MINDSET

1. When have you been so desperate to get a yes that you agreed to bad business? What was the outcome?
2. Think of a time that you said no to something that didn't make sense. How did you feel after?
3. Is there something that you need to walk away from? What limiting beliefs are holding you back from saying no?

## SHIFTABILITY ACTION

Are there some deals in your funnel that are getting stale? Try a peer-coaching model for doing a Deal Review or Funnel Health Review. The intent is to have shoulder-to-shoulder conversations with impartial peers who can help you evaluate the health of your business opportunities. Ask these questions:

1. What specific actions or decisions have happened recently?
2. What hasn't happened? What deadline was missed or pushed out? What meeting was cancelled?
3. Are you still acting but the client's decision-making process has stalled?

# Ten

# Shifting Into What's Next

The future always arrives too fast... and in the wrong order.

*ALVIN TOFLER*

The future started yesterday and we're already late.

*JOHN LEGEND*

The future depends on what we do in the present.

*MAHATMA GANDHI*

he world has changed. We all agree. But perhaps the bigger challenge before us is not just adapting and responding to the present changes, but figuring out how to continuously adapt to constant change and flux. Rapid change is now the constant we can depend on. Just when we figure out the "next new thing" it's already a thing of the past. This is true for everyone, but the age of change and disintermediation seems to be particularly harsh for the sales professional.

We believe that future success in selling depends on personal change and transformation, not just adopting a new sales technique. And we believe that the shiftability mindset and skillset we have described in this book are central to successful transformation.

In wrapping this up, we want to quickly recap our answers to the three central questions every good sales professional has to answer:

**Why change?**
**Why change now?**
**Why change to what we are offering you?**

In this case, the *why change* is the realization and acceptance that the pervasive access of information has forever changed the role of the B2B sales professional. Where once we were needed to supply information, we are now needed for something much greater. This is a reality that way too many sales people have not yet accepted and they are still doing the same things they have always done and expecting different outcomes. You have to learn a new way to operate in this new reality.

*Why now*, is simple. If you don't shift now you will become obsolete in the near future. You will be joining T-Rex and the other dinosaurs in the museum. The rate of change is picking up, not slowing down and it's only going to get harder. Make no mistake – this is not a seasonal shift; this is a seismic shaking of the way things will work from now on.

The *why to what we are offering* is also simple – to engage the change in our context in a meaningful way in any frame requires that we embrace personal transformation as the primary step. Shiftability is the personal potential anyone can exercise to transform themselves into meaningful contributors to a dynamic environment.

The good news is that there are a handful of sales thought leaders that are in sync and are developing and talking about a rising tide of change. Dave Brock (Partners in Excellence blog) and Anthony Innarino (The Sales Blog) have talked about the fundamental issue that we are holding up here as our reason for WHY. It is centered around the concept that as an individual, or a company, you are well served to understand, create, and communicate what it is that makes you different from everyone else, and why the client should bother to spend any time talking to you. While once you could rely on the features and benefits of your products, the mass commoditization of both information and products demands something different. Great products are now table stakes. It is now up to the individual to create differentiation – differentiation that is specific to each client that they serve along the decision-making journey.

And the challenging part of this new thinking is that this new client engagement style must also shift easily to accommodate all of the unknown variables that the rapidly changing world will continue to throw at us. We must create a capability that shifts as needed to respond to the world. That requires a foundation of shiftability at its core. Only this kind of thinking will insure that we understand each new challenge and that we respond in kind with new thinking that matches it.

The shiftability mindset and skillset at the core creates the understanding of why and how we can think differently, believe differently, and act differently. Only that realization and action will keep us relevant in a universe that has a rate of change that is greater every day than it was the day before.

These are timeless abilities and skills, which will transcend the trends and ideas of the moment and establish a sustainable competitive advantage in selling. We believe that if you cultivate the shiftability mindset and skillset you will be equipped to thrive in sales today – and tomorrow. And the day after. And the day after that.

# Acknowledgements

*From Mitch*

The work of many people has fed the story that we tell. I want to thank a few of the key people in my life that have helped me to see things "different". My coach and friend Steve Chandler showed me by example how the power of truly listening in pure absorption mode could change the world. He taught me to be Fearless. At Microchip I have worked for one man for 27 years, Steve Sanghi. This Steve taught me the true meaning of "walking the talk" and again the power of listening in inquiry mode and never judging. Probably the singular most intelligent person I have the pleasure of knowing is Brent Adamson. Through his work at the CEB Brent has shone the light on new ways of seeing information in the selling arena that will forever change my world and through the work we do pass along that change to the bigger world. Dan Pink's work in *Drive* proves that sales people are not coin-operated and has given us all the understanding of personal motivation that allows us to challenge the status quo thinking about how to really build leading sales teams. My partner in all of this work is Hendre. I have seen him coach and communicate with hundreds of individuals over the years. Hendre connects with the heart and soul and it is a beautiful thing to see happen. He is the best!

*From Hendre*

There are so many friends, company leaders and individual clients that have trusted me with the moments of their greatest opportunity and the dark nights of their soul. Without your trust and invitation I would not get to do the work I love. Thank you – I am forever grateful and thankful for your contribution to my life and for the privilege to stand with you.

This book truly is the result of the fun and powerful work that I get to do with Mitch Little and his team at Microchip. Mitch, you sir, are an inspiration, a tireless giver and an incredible leader. I have not witnessed any other leader invest so much in the formation and development of their team as you. The way you are moved when people get a breakthrough in their thinking and skill development is truly a testament of how much you care. Your relentless discipline and willingness to delegate and empower others is an example to us all. Thank you that we get to do this book together!

*From Both*
And THANK YOU to Jennifer Zach, who is the true power of the pen behind our words here. Her guidance, creativity, and connection are a marvel to witness.

Thank you all. You have made this great!

*Mitch & Hendre*

# About the Authors

Mitch Little and Hendre Coetzee have been leading and coaching sales professionals throughout the world to success and relevance for many years. Through their work with thousands of people they have firsthand experience with trying out the latest thinking and ideas, discovering what really works (and what doesn't) and figuring out some of the missing pieces. Along the way they have gained some important insights about the nature of selling and what will be required for continued success for sales professionals and ultimately the companies they represent. Mitch and Hendre's book is grounded in their real life experience of working in the trenches of business-to-business complex sales.

## MITCH LITTLE
**Vice President, Worldwide Sales and Applications, Microchip Technology Inc.**

With over four decades years in the electronics industry Mitch Little has led global engineering, marketing and sales teams both small and large, startup and mature. He has been a part of Microchip Technology since 1989 and now leads the worldwide sales and applications team of the $10+ Billion market cap company. In the fall of 2015, Microchip posted its 100th consecutive quarter of profitability, a record unmatched by any other company in the industry.

Mitch has a Bachelor's of Science - Electronic Technology degree. Since joining Microchip Technology in 1989 he has held several Vice President positions in product line and sales leadership and is a Section 16 Officer of the company. He has been Vice President of Worldwide Sales and Application Engineering since July 2000, leading the only non-commissioned sales team in the industry. In 2006 he won the Worldwide VP of the Year Sales Award from Selling Power Magazine. For three years in a row, Microchip Technology has been recognized as one of the TOP 50 companies to sell for by Selling Power magazine.

Mitch is a member of the CEB Sales Advisory Board, a select group of Chief Sales Officers representing leading companies including Kaiser Permanente, Disney, and Fidelity Investments. He is also a Certified Master Coach with the Behavioral Coaching Institute, a member of the Executive Advisory Board for Model N, and a past Vice President of the Board of Directors of the Upward Foundation.

## HENDRE COETZEE
**Futurist, Transformation Specialist and Global Leader in Neuroscience Based Immersive Coaching, Founder of the Center for Advanced Coaching, Co-founder of Virtu Partners**

Hendre Coetzee is a Transformation Specialist. His work as speaker and executive coach has allowed him to address executives, boards, teams and entire organizations on the subjects of Transformation and Change, Unlocking Potential and Resilience.

He has over 20 years of experience within the corporate domain, realms of social justice, non-profit and relief and development work across the globe. He has provided transformational work in over 50 countries and has guest lectured at a number of universities including the Harvard Faculty Club multiple times on the Neuroscience of Change and Transformation.

From 2013 through 2016, Hendre was selected as one of the Top 25 Business and Executive Coaches to speak at the World Business & Executive

Coach Summit, joining a roster including John Maxwell, Ken Blanchard, Marshall Goldsmith and Judith Glaser.

Hendre's experience varies from working as a facilitator for the integration between black and white youth in post-Apartheid South Africa, to negotiating mergers for large financial institutions and developing performance-training modules for High Performing Traders on the NYSE and NASDAQ.

Whether as Keynote Speaker, Workshop Facilitator or working 1:1 as an Executive Coach with a C-Suite Leader his commitment is to unlock people's potential, co-design a clear path forward and move them into momentum.

His clients have included Microchip Technology, API, Disney, ESPN, Estee Lauder, Revlon, New York Life, FedEx and Compassion International.

# Connect

Please stay in touch. We welcome hearing your stories and how you are creating a sustainable advantage in selling. Send us an email, visit our websites and connect with us:

mitch@shiftability.com          hendre@shiftability.com
www.mitchlittle.com             www.hendrecoetzee.com
Twitter: @mitchlittle1          Twitter: @HendreCoetzee

Interested in bringing *Shiftability* to your team or organization?
Visit www.shiftability.com.

Made in the USA
San Bernardino, CA
28 February 2017